SEER I

Keys to our Divine Nature As Multi-Dimensional Creator Beings of the Light

Maraya Forrest

Contents

7

8

A NOTE TO THE READER

Dear Reader,

These writings are simply a guide to your own self discovery. They are a record of my personal experience of becoming multi-dimensional and my understanding of aspects of consciousness materialised into form within this plane of existence. I encourage you to willingly apply yourself in gaining your own inner understanding of your true nature through your own process. I encourage self realisation of your unique gifts and potential, as well as higher levels of self empowerment and alignment to embody these designs in consciousness. It is within this earthly dimension and density that we are learning to create and materialise. It is here where the foundation of loving ourselves as creation and the magic of creating a life that we love, begins.

A GUIDE TO USING THIS BOOK

THIS BOOK IS MY understanding of how consciousness materialises into form. The designs of home on earth.

It is a compilation of stories about the divine nature of our creator's heart. How the nature of his spirit materialises into form. It contains keys to understanding our true nature reflected in mother nature, and maintained by the laws of nature. We have had many lifetimes experiencing these patterns and studying these designs. I wrote these stories to gain a deeper understanding of myself.

When we understand mother earth and all life upon her, we understand ourselves, our divine nature. Her landscapes are the landscapes of our consciousness, her creatures are characters or characteristics that are parts of ourselves, her plants hold the gifts that we are uniting with in order to know her as ourselves. We are here to unite with her and experience her as an expression of ourselves.

These stories are my experience of some of her designs, an impression of my consciousness here.

You too can have your own experience of her by simply breathing deeply and relaxing into any pattern, coming to know and understand your personal truth of each part of your divine nature.

One can read this book in any order by simply going to the aspect you relate to and would like to connect and gain a deeper understanding of. Everything is connected. It may also be used for dream analysis, understanding visions or feelings encountered in applied meditation or breathwork, or simply as a reflection of everyday life.

If the soul came to the planet to learn, how does it see itself, but in the mirror. Should you encounter a tortoise on the road, it may benefit you to reflect upon this part of your nature that has materialised itself in order to be seen and remembered. Become conscious of the characters or characteristics that you are drawn to understanding, within yourself. As you read the stories you are potentially aligning yourself to those parts that resonate with an inner truth, and this has infinite potential for you to explore.

Please note that because the stories are a multi-dimensional experience, you will notice that at some point the storyteller becomes the expression of 'I'. This is when the embodiment of an aspect is speaking.

It may also be helpful to begin by grounding and balancing yourself with either your own meditation or the guided one on my website. This may also assist with aligning you within the timelines and dimensions of your own experience and wisdom, orienting you for your souls forward evolution.

Introduction

Heaven and Earth - *consciousness in form*

Within the heart are the DNA of the continents, our creation as earth. Surrounding the heart are the feelings, the oceans supporting the continents. These feelings hold the pieces of ourselves together, the lifetimes of experience in different timelines on the different continents here upon the earth. Above the continents and the oceans is the air, our breath connecting us to life here on earth. The light, our spirit descends into this place warming and expanding life here. We are this light of creation uniting with the earth herself, through our breath and emotions to finally settle into our hearts and remember ourselves as Earth. Bringing our gifts to this place to connect and co-create.

The Light

Within the unseen light of day fall the codes of creation in sacred designs, to be received by those hearts that are willing and open, trusting hearts.

Within the knowing heart is guidance leading the way home, one step at a time. One step at a time.

Within the incoming flow of light from on high, are sacred symbols seeking a place to position themselves, to land and merge, and to materialise into a glow. These patterns hold the signature frequencies of lands far away, lands of golden wheat gently undulating under a golden sun.

Even when a dark carriage rides along a dusty road, the light symbols fall graciously through its darkness to settle upon the earth. Each symbol is a voice, a pattern, a song of creation, a gift from the heavens. These symbols rain upon the earth, showers of golden light with crystalline protection, vibrating with shimmering ideologies, clarity, transparency and diamond resilience.

The green welcoming nature of life on earth continuously expands with these designs. A sacred symbol on a green leaf boldly shifts the crystalline light above the leaf creating patterns within the crystal clear air; and then uniting with each other as they land; a web of design, a web of protection, a web of perfection.

The simple green leaf has a central vein of flow connected to many arteries, and each leaf is connected to the tree. The Tree of Life, our key story and design.

A distant snow capped mountain on the horizon to the North, overseas the birthing of fresh green leaves on the trees under crystal clear blue skies, under the golden glow of the sun. Each leaf a heart pumping life force to the tree, the strength of the tree as powerful as the heart holding its love.

The Materialisation of Form

The light of creation is available to all Creator Beings. The light of our creator's heart can be seen materialised into form in mother nature. This light has little characters in it, the elemental kingdom or nature spirits. We call this light the Holy Spirit as it is an expression of the nature of the spirit of our Creator's heart.

The creators of Form as seen in nature on earth are the mighty Elohim, and the blueprint design of our universe can be seen materialised into form in the nature kingdom. The Elohim command the light within the laws of nature, creating form under the guidance of the Devic Kingdom and the Elemental Kingdom.

As each of our individual light unites with the earth-plane, we connect to the golden grids of light remembering ourselves and our experiences through all of the timelines and landscapes of our consciousness upon her. We bring our gifts and knowledge from within this universe and beyond, uniting and expanding with her. Golden light materialises into gold, and this is Mother Earth's wealth and her expansive power of connection and protection.

Earth's Astrology symbol

In order to connect to the golden grids of light and expand our consciousness into all of the timelines and dimensions that we are experiencing here, we need to balance each of our chakras into the cross in the circle. This means we need to bring our lower four bodies into balance - physical, emotional, mental and spiritual.

As our chakras balance into the cross in the circle, we become a vertical stream of light. Each chakra connects into the golden grids and we become multi-dimensional. Our connection to the grids expands our consciousness and we are able to remember what we are learning from our lifetimes in the different lines of time here. This is our wisdom, the gold, from our experiences here upon earth.

Our astrological earth symbol, the cross in the circle includes: the four directions which hold our light stream within the space/time continuum; the four elements which bring form into being - earth, water, air and fire; and the lower four bodies, which we need to bring into balance in order to align ourselves onto the golden grids, where **earth** is the physical body, **water** is the emotional body, **air** is the mental body and **fire** is the spirit body. These four elements make up the existence of our material world. As we bring these lower four bodies into balance, we align and unite each of our unique soul signature frequencies with the patterning of the Great Mother, Mother Nature, uniting heaven and earth.

The landscapes of Mother Earth are the landscapes of our consciousness.

Understanding our true nature is to understand her designs seen materialised into form in her nature, creatures, seasons and landscapes. As we unite with her we experience the expressions of her divine nature as our own. With courage always leading the way, for to move from fear to love takes courage and one might say that this is our central theme of study. Remembering to trust in our true nature, the patterns of the creation of this universe in form.

The below writings are keys to the creational process in the form of characters, archetypes, stories and the earth's landscapes as expressions of our divine nature.

1

IN THE BEGINNING

In the beginning within the eternal empty dark space of existence the first spark of light came into being, and then began to multiply into divine patterns of perfection. Through the space of time the sparks of light could be seen to form different shapes, and thus the spirit of the Creator configured within the space. Each design contained the Creator's intended purpose, each with their own unique gift and talent possessing the very nature and existence of the Creator. Shining forth with brilliant light and design. Each individual design held a pattern, a form with an energy, respectively an expression of creation in its purest form.

The wolf, naturally a vicious protector, began to look for something to protect, the elephant began to look for something to move from its path, and the crocodile watched with deep absorption the essence of all that surrounded it.

In the centre of these star-lit patterns was the exquisite Temple of Silence. And deep from within the Silence began the harmonic sounds of creation. The combinations of chords in chorus sang forth into the empty spaces between the stars, connecting them in bright colours. A pulse, a heartbeat, sweetly gently began to emanate from the Temple's centre.

Each form began to respond to the colours and sounds, and then to one another, simply living out their individual natures as the creator had intended them. Some intuitively avoided each other whilst others enjoyed and learned from one another, evolving in consciousness yet still true to their inherent nature.

Father Creator guided his reindeer and sleigh through this universe of creation, enjoying the development of relation between the characters and the way that they were interacting and learning from each other. He noticed that an awareness was growing between the different characters and that they were watching one another, learning from each other respectfully. This pleased him. He returned to the Temple and began to play another tune. From this melody spirals of light sprang forth in circles and cycles, appearing as flowers.

Within a cycle and circle far away from the temple, within a sphere of light where the heartbeat was very slow, these patterns of the stars began to take form and materialise. Where they had once roamed freely in the space of eternity, they now had a surface upon which to travel. The young deer nourished itself from the leaves of the trees and the grasses of the lands, always smelling the flowers and being aware of the blue, blue skies above. This was the earth plane. The crocodile who had always watched and absorbed with awareness that which surrounded him, felt connected to the flow of everything. And so he brought this connection of flow with him to the earth plane, and lived within the flow of the rivers. The flight of the birds were connected to the lightness of being, and responded to the sounds around them in song. They answered from the purist space within their hearts, gliding upon the streams of light between materialised trees. And within each tree was a spiral of energy flowing upwards, pulsing forth from the heartbeat in the very centre of the sphere. The heart of the sphere was connected in slow unison to the Temple far away.

The earth herself not only echoed the heartbeat of creation so far away, she also emitted a song of her own which she gently emanated outwards in response to the sounds that she was receiving. Her song was a song of love, a love of simply being. Being able to hold all of this life upon her as part of her. It brought her immense joy. The awareness continued to grow and harmony prevailed in the warmth of the sun, the light of creation. Life on earth had begun, the completion of the materialisation of form from the sparks of the stars.

Within the rivers of light the flow of connection and awareness continued to evolve, including awareness of that which is separate from self. The earth separate from the breeze, the breeze separate from the movement of the flowers and trees. And everything separate from the clear blue skies above. The mountains reflected the form of the Creator's many faces of wisdom. The ocean felt the warmth of the sun upon her surface, with shifting currents and depths of connection beneath. This infinite awareness of existence and connection continually deepening and expanding.

Forces of creation within the patterns of existence moved closer to the earth, emanating their love and their unique gifts into the sphere, into this realm of Being. They transmitted their love to her, also receiving an understanding of relationship. Whilst their relationship was with the earth herself, upon the earth the other relationships continued to evolve. There was increasing awareness between each and all of these designs and expressions of consciousness, which pulsated all the way back to the Temple of the Creator, to the beat of his heart.

...and as the song of a bird sang out into the universe, from afar a harmonic chord responded, each question being answered, each answer being sung.

But the earth was moving away from the heart of the creator and was now halfway into the eternal darkness of space.

The Temple was calling her back...and so she responded with her heart, 'Creator pull me gently back into the circle of your light for I am on the edge and the darkness is confusing.' Using her will power she told her children to find the rainbows of light. To connect to the flow of light that is creation and return towards the Temple of Light and Sound. To become encircled within His love, once again.

2

THE GARDEN OF EDEN

The Story of Our Divine Nature in the Garden

WITHIN THE GARDEN OF each of our creations exists the patterns of our original design, the tree of life, the flower of life, the fruit of life and the seed of life. The fruits hang from the trees sweet and fragrant ready for absorption, their sweet nourishment satiating our deep hunger. The garden grows under the blue skies of heaven on earth as a natural expression of her existence, abundant and wild. The flowing designs are rooted into the earth and naturally reach for the light, stretching themselves upwards, growing in strength in order to stand firm and steady. Some are vines and cling to others, whilst others are mighty trees anchored, balanced and resilient. And under the clear blue skies within the unseen warmth of the sunlight, exist many unseen designs waiting to materialise.

Like the heart chakra the garden is primarily green, absorbing the light and nurturing and nourishing itself, coexistence between the plants an interplay of creation. This paradise on earth is our natural state of being here. It is that which we are experiencing and learning from as an experience of self. Heaven and Earth uniting.

The Story of Our Divine Nature in the Garden

I open my heart as a **flower** to the light of my soul, receiving all that I am in the knowing that I am the light of God, I am so loved, I am the beloved. I receive this love in my heart and then I begin to blossom. Through my willingness to receive this light that I am, I am able to bloom creating the sweet nectar of love, the very core and nature of my being.

From this place, I bear the **fruits** of my labours being able to receive the fruits that are sweet and juicy; life in its fullest expression of abundance and pleasure. The joyful expression of a creative heart's fulfilment.

And then by planting the **seeds** from the fruit, these seeds that are creations of love, and gently watering them, I bring the Creator's qualities of the light to my existence. I am able to embody the Kingdoms of Heaven.

From these seeds birth another **tree**, standing tall and still holding onto its consciousness with deep roots. The depth of the roots of the tree into the dark fertile soils below, determine the height of its branches reaching into the heavens on high. No two trees are ever the same, even from the same family. Such is the nature of life on earth in this garden of paradise.

Winter - The Tree

The Tree of Life - *As above so below*

The medium sized tree is filled with fresh green leaves, its roots weaving both above and below the ground. The roots are seeking oxygen before their natural descent into the dark soils below. The earth below is compact, lacking air and moisture which the tree knows it needs. The roots below the ground are deep and branch outwards for stability, pressing their way into and through the dark soils.

Upon the surface of the earth, between above and below, between the light and the dark, a measured balance exists, connecting the worlds. Above, is spacious light and freedom for expansion, whilst below, is the counterbalance. This place in-between is where we learn about co-existence and equilibrium.

Within the central column of the tree is a portal of flow, steady and true. It feeds the different designs of above and below as needed, and is perpetually receiving and transmitting.

The heartbeat of the tree is synced to the thrum of the earth's heartbeat, uniting it to the pulse of life that is the whole. This steady beat allows the tree to reach up towards the light, the rhythm flowing upwards and outwards; sending messages in translation. Prayers for that which the earth and soil are lacking, prayers to be heard and answered within the returning light. The light always responds with codes of perfection which the tree then receives, its green leaves absorbing the light frequencies and converting it into nourishment and nurture.

The inner tube of the tree is an open space of flow and connection, messages passing up and down through the heart. The heart also flows outwards in horizontal frequencies with messages to life surrounding it. And so, the vertical-horizontal balance is brought into being, creating a sphere of perfection around the tree. This appears as an orb, an expression of the divine perfectly balanced between the light and the dark.

The Green Leaf - *the heart*

 A single firm green leaf, alone but attached. The stem is small and soft compared to the thick grey-brown branch. The leaf's only apparent function is to receive the light and feed the tree.

The pink, soft veined human heart is connected in a flow of light that enters from above and descends into the earth, into the body.

In expression of the heart are the hands that create from within this flow as well as the space from which the voice sounds, the ears listen to the movement around the body, and the scents alert the senses. And as the feet carry this body, this flow of light that moves hither and thither, it is always a communication interface between above and below.

The steady pulse of the soft fleshy heart holds the same function as the soft green leaf on the tree. To feed the branches, the body and the roots of the tree.

Our human hands bring into expression the dream in our heart, and are the creators of material existence. They bring into expression the outward flow from the heart. It is the heart which builds and creates, and from which spirals of energy receive and transmit to the higher realms. The ears are the same. The central column through the mind, the heart and the perineum centre bring vertical balance to the horizontal flow through the hands. This energetic cross connects the body to the grids of light that connect each individual to the whole. And each heart is a point of being, pulsing the energetic flow both vertically and horizontally in connecting spheres of light. All work individually and together. This is co-creation upon the earthplane. It is the hands sowing the seeds of existence.

For in truth all is already here. Mother nature has provided her perfection, we simply plant and nurture that which already is. That we might nourish ourselves with it, and experience life here.

The Ancestral Tree - *embodying the light of our ancestors*

Our family tree is our lineage that descends in consciousness to embody upon earth. This is the light, the wisdom that we embody.

The green leaves move freely in a gentle breeze. They are attached to a tree under a clear blue sky and connect the light to the earth. They are green hearts of loving reception, and the heart is the pulse of its universe.

A green leaf on a tree is translucent in the morning sunlight, fresh and newly generated. Slowly with age it darkens and thickens as it strengthens itself to the elements surrounding it. It remains firmly attached to the tree until seasons end.

A singular small leaf on a very large tree is at times held within the deep stillness of a breathless day but at other times blown relentlessly within dire circumstances. It only manages to stay attached to the tree through its heart's intention. In an unremitting wind that does its utmost to clear everything in its path with its intention to shift old patterns and open space for the new; the dear souls billow in the storm, stretched to the limit.

Within the dark empty stillness of an expansive night sky, when the stars appear so very far away and with so much space in between, there is space for the arrival of the new. New designs of perfection. Pathways and trails can be seen in the night sky, evidence of the soul song of each unique star's light-stream. A mighty elephant leads the way strolling slowly in front of each soul choosing to follow. Tunnels of crystalline arteries connecting the destiny of hearts on the path.

The soft fleshy veins of life on the green leaf extend outwards from its central spine, in a flow of connection. Each leaf is a heart, a pulse of life feeding the tree, nourishing its enormous body and roots. The leaves are so small and fragile and yet so powerful in their function, without which, the tree cannot survive. It is the very light of its soul.

The Tree of Illumination

With an umbrella of illuminated leaves, and beyond, a star filled sky. Each leaf is a heavenly body of creation glowing into the surrounding darkness. Rainbow veins of light course down her body, embedding themselves into the earth, above, her fingers reaching towards the heavens, hands open to receive.

She whispers her song into the universe who responds in turn with love, answering the call of her heart.

Her roots deepen into the dark soils below, her rainbow body a stream of perfection in the empty space surrounding her.

Her hands hold mounds of diamonds, refractions of patterns streaming forth in every direction creating lines of connection between heaven and earth.

The ears of the elementals receive her song in the wind and race towards her in wonder and awe. With hands covering their mouths in amazement they watch her illuminate life surrounding her, her light extending in every direction, Her roots ever deepening into the dark soils, her leaves shimmering brilliantly.

Serpentine roots submerge into the Great Mother's welcoming embrace, into the cave of her heart of darkness, that she might illuminate her world.

Spring - The Flower

The Flower - *opening our heart to the light of our creation*

The Daisy

The soft pink flesh of the human heart pulses steadily, its beat supporting the expression of its song. Blue veins protrude from the translucent lining of tissue covering it; rivers and estuaries of life.

Within the heart's interior is a bright yellow daisy with a dark furry centre. It supports a honey bee seeking sweet nectar, the bee is buzzing with joy and delight. The honey bee thanks the flower for her gift, and then disappears into the light blue ethereal skies.

The dark, furry centre of the flower moves in subtle pulses, responding to its world that is a night sky. This world consists of an empty flow of space between the stars, subtle frequencies of the unknown, the unseen. Gently, rhythmically the daisy draws the furry points inwards, in circular ripples of response. The distance between the ripples is a reflection of the unseen night, the centre points closing together, tips trustingly embracing in exquisite delight.

A ring of thirteen yellow petals spills vibrantly from the edge of the textured centre. Upon a petal on the right side, a drop of water balances reflecting a neighbouring yellow daisy.

The daisy's long green stem extends downwards towards the ground, firmly securing the upright position of the flower, deep roots embedded into the soil. Above, a blue, clear sky with deep undulating waves of ever shifting energies reaches down towards this singular life form on the earth-plane, the connection unseparated.

This little yellow flower so small and seemingly insignificant, stands upon the rolling green hills of the heart which extend to the blue mountains of the North. To the West, the golden yellow sun is finally setting, with a deep, peaceful sigh of content for days end. The daisy responds by swaying in the gentle breeze of its breath, so very appreciative of this long day passed.

Above, a flock of storks fly towards the East.

The Pink Hibiscus of the Heart - *opening the heart through trust and balance*

An open, vibrantly pink hibiscus flower with bright green receptacle and stem. This is the wide open, blossoming higher heart supported by its centre and stem. The stem leads down towards the ground where the flower's roots reach deeply into the soil, supporting its structure in a potential breeze.

The pink petals expand outwards from its intense red centre, the centre providing a solid backdrop to the golden yellow powdery stamens that greet the sun. The pollen from the stamens wafts into the air onto unseen patterns within light streams, summoning life to draw nearer. Breathless golden-yellow materialised molecules floating outward upon unseen designs of perfection, creating a warm, joyful glow.

The honeybee recognises this light from afar, its enticing scent bringing the promise of great joy. The reflection of golden light is warm and inviting.

The masculine structure of the stem stands to attention with its anther extended, golden bobbles of beauty at the tip.

The deep red of the flower's inner petals are shiny and smooth with a membrane of filmy protection for the heart of the blooming flower. The softer green upper stem, luminous with life, a passageway to the earth's gifts from below. This combination of green and pink echoes the undulating hills in the setting sun at closing of the day.

The Lotus Flower - *emotionally opening the heart*

Om Mani Pad me Hum - I Am the jewel in the Lotus Flower.

With serpent-like roots stretching downwards through clear water, emotions of clarity, they seek to latch into the earth, fingers grasping for something firm. At first they encounter slippery mud and have no solid grip, but with deeper seeking they sink into the darkness of the earth below. If we seek within the buried feelings of the unknown, and if we trust whilst we seek in that darkness, there are embedded crystalline jewels within the earth. Deep knowing within our body. For within our bodies as part of creation, are the crystalline jewels. It is the earth's natural design, our bodies' natural design.

We can trust this process of creation, it is a natural flow of the Divine.

As the root of the flower hungrily clasps the embedded jewels deep within the earth's body, the light of the jewels' crystalline nature connects to the root. This connection between the earth and this flower within our heart, is a natural process. For within the earth, within our bodies, are jewels of wisdom and unique light frequencies.

Each jewel is held within mother earth, within the design of her perfection as a part of her creation. The light pink crystals emanate both love and compassion, sapphires are a reflection of the heavens on high, and the golden yellow crystals hold the wisdom of the light of our soul.

Within each of our hearts is this design of the lotus flower yearning to awaken to the daylight at the birthing of each new day; each new idea, each new journey. Some are blue, some are pink and some are yellow, growing on still waters where their reflection is clear. Their reflection being a result of the sun's journey across the sky, as they float on the water connected to all surrounding life.

The Sunflower - *Opening the heart to receive the love of the divine father*

The nature of the sunflower is to follow the sun, the light of the soul, and to absorb light encodings through her golden-yellow petals. She allows the flow of this knowledge to stream down to her roots and into the soil and then she draws up wisdom from the soil, producing loads of seeds. She is perfectly balanced between heaven and earth. She then releases those seeds abundantly onto the landscape.

The sun was gone and the sunflowers head hung sorrowfully.

Her thick green stem was prickly with protection and her heart lacked the will to connect to the ever illuminating star filled sky. She felt the light of the stars shining on the back of her neck encouraging her to find hope and lift her face to the light once more. But she felt tired and whilst she listened to their voices, the sadness in her heart flowed from her eyes. Only inner willingness and deep breaths of re-connection would enable a strong flow through her, that might straighten her spine and proudly raise her head.

Deep inside she was feeling sorry for herself and it would take willpower to reconnect to her purpose.

As she rested in that semi-conscious relaxed space of weariness, the many voices of the stars began to flow together becoming a harmonic chorus of sound. She could no longer hear their individual voices, only their united musical harmonies of intention. The sounds awakened the night crickets on the ground who in turn united to respond with a voice of their own.

The sound of the chords from the stars appeared as threads of light travelling towards the earth. Forgetting her woes for a moment, she focused on the undulating light threads, some wispy others more demanding. At first the threads of light were white in colour, but the more she concentrated on tuning into them, their separate colours became apparent. Crystalline pinks of loving compassion, heavenly blues of empowerment and those that crossed each other became violet flames of transmutation. The golden-yellow rays of hope and joy were higher up. There were also emerald greens of her heart, mother nature.

She raised her head to the rising crescent moon just above the horizon to the East, feeling grandmother moon's message to her - that she must receive and contain the chords; to become a chalice for this light. With a heavy sadness in her heart still present, she focused upon the moon and her message. With every in-breath, she noticed that she started to become a cup of receptivity. Grateful for being here, rooted and grounded under the perfection of the patterns of the stars, with a clear view of the crescent moon rising over the horizon.

She became aware of her warm golden-yellow petals, soft and delicate, a source of integration for her seeds of creation. Her large green furry leaves were hearts of productivity, transforming the light into food to nourish and nurture her body. Her roots extended into the comforting soils that supported her, so that she might grow tall and stand strong. She became more aware of herself and in appreciation of her design.

The infinite blue skies above and her devotional nature always to seek the light of the sun and to follow his path across the skies. She spent her nights listening to the ensemble on high, harmonies of perfection and escalation. She became aware of this short season of hers, before her body would return to the earth once more.

The Vine - *co-dependence and independence*

A bright translucent green vine lay on the forest floor with nothing nearby to cling to, that it might quickly grow up towards the light. It is beginning to entangle into itself using its energy to coil and weave inwards. It becomes a floppy green intertwined circle. Slowly, it grows higher on its own, having no support from around it, simply balancing on top of itself. And thus it builds a structure of strength from within, without clinging to something outside of itself.

Holding on to a structure would assist a vine to climb to greater heights quickly, as a single stem in a symbiotic relationship. A single vine climbing up a tall and powerful tree with its little tentacles embedded into the rough bark, might cling to the tree's structure using it as a firm, deeply rooted foundation. Attaching itself to the majestic tree enables a swift and sturdy ascent towards the light above the forest.

The vine, alone on the floor, slowly grows higher, needing to constantly extend new roots into the earth in order to stabilise its base. As it weaves its way into itself, it becomes stronger and stronger, ascending higher and higher.

The singular vine on the tree only has one set of roots that can easily be severed by a gnawing worm with large teeth and no consideration.

The nature of the coiled vine is to grow in a circle spiralling upwards towards the light, its many roots holding it in place.

The vine finally reaches the light at the top of the forest spreading itself horizontally over the treetops. Parts of it drape over and dangle down into the cool shade. This is symbiosis.

Heavenly Blue Morning Glory - *open hearted optimism*

The deep indigo blue flower lay open on the cold cement floor, her cheerful nature contrasting the stark environment. She was attached to a vine that had crawled into the house from the exterior, seeking warmth and shelter from the elements. Her ability to adjust to both environments revealed her strength, as she stretched herself forwards in search of new earth, to root. Her ability to find a path across cold, barren landscapes void of life, in hopes of something new to ground into or potentially climb. Always in awe at the possibility of crispy fresh air under the sparkly blue heavens, her heart open to the light of the infinite.

The Magic of the Flower of Life, Universal - *The structure of the DNA and how it connects to the timelines*

The full moon shimmered, showering her light upon the night sky. Her gift and glorious love of peering into the unknown. Within her glow hung threads of light upon which little beings swung, singing their songs of truth, their stories, their tales of perception. A pixie like figure dangled upon a lit twine, pointing persuasively out towards the stars in the North East; the exact timeline 13.06. He was requesting assistance from the designs in this cycle.

Instantaneously, upon the earth-plane emerged a lone figure riding his bicycle. The spokes of the wheels appeared as cycles and circles of time moving forward. He rode across a desert landscape moving West towards a square terracotta adobe building. Behind the building descended the fiery golden ball mercilessly onto the horizon, imminent completion of a long day. The figure hurried frantically towards his destination, before darkness could envelop him.

Within the sandy building were tables filled with magical artefacts all bristling to come into action, expecting to burst into expression of the purpose for which they had been created. Each artefact carried magical powers, designs embedded into materialised form. They possessed the spirits and wisdom of their ancestors, the magicians that had created them.

The man from the bicycle ran into the building, now softly lit with golden light. He urgently propelled his way towards the third table from the door, the second table from the back wall. Seizing a miniature stone face that resembled those beings of Rapa Nui, he began to speak with it in hushed tones as he hurried out of the building into the empty desert night sky.

He was commiserating, telling a story of his misfortune, whilst he simultaneously aligned his heart with the frequency of the little figure. He came into prayer sharing the woes of his heart, and then with a deep breath exhaled and arrived in silence. For he knew that within this empty space of silence, he would receive the answers to the prayer of his heart. He would hear the solution to the story of this miserable creation tormenting him, and how to illuminate this suffering. How to embrace the teachings of that which he had learned from this experience and gain understanding and find deep peace and acceptance within his centre.

Slowly within the recesses of his brain, within the distant past of his existence, within the long forgotten memories hidden in the dark unseen world of his consciousness, a song emerged from within the silence. A song of the Great Mother.

Encircling him, geometric flowers of light and balance appeared, wrapping him in glowing patterns of illumination. With himself in the centre of a flower, he saw elemental beings carrying their songs in threads of light, waves of light pulsing up into the darkness around the building, and stretching as far into the empty desert landscape as the eye could see.

Each Being was connected to the stars and emanated the frequencies of its original purpose. They transmitted with their voices, expressions of the very nature of their existence into the still night air.

Before him lay the mirror of Above. The reflection of his soul in his original design. He was the light of the patterns in the night sky, in the designs of a flower, in circles and cycles of time and space.

These circles of magical Beings, each holding a candle and chanting in unison, were the holy spirit of the fire, the light of the stars. And in the dark spaces in between - where there was nothing, lay the emptiness of his soul.

He willed himself to connect to the sound of the chant and focused on the light from the fires held in the hands of each chanting Being. And then with the flow of truth timeless, the rhythm of the story began to move through him.

'Child of God, image of mine, open your heart to the song-lines of the whales. Remember swimming with them to the far North where you met the Giants and they encoded you with their memories, their wisdom. Allow this wisdom to return, the wisdom of the planet, your body so long ago. Allow the frozen patterns and designs to dissolve into your consciousness that you might remember yourself as Creation, as Creator. Every step you have chosen, every decision you have made has been to assist you to return to this place of remembering. Let go of resistance and fear. Allow your true nature to return.'

He looked at the circle of light surrounding him with extending petals. He saw the many centres of many flowers all spinning in cycles and circles of connection. Each cycle a story, a timeline of existence here on the earthplane. He allowed himself to become the dark tunnel of the centre of the flower where he stood, moving through time and space, until he looked into the eternity of his Creator's eyes, and recognised himself. I Am.

And then abruptly he was back upon the earth plane, the light and the song slowly receding. His heart deeply peaceful in the sacred wisdom of the eternal. Standing alone under the night sky, the cold little stone figure in his hand, appearing as an ordinary object.

Summer - The Fruit

The Fruit of Life - *becoming receptive, receiving the fruits of your labours.*

Within the sweet juicy fruits are the seeds of new creation containing potential new growth.

The golden crown sits upon the young girl's head and she enjoys the delicious taste and aroma of the fruits.

At the harbour a mermaid awaits the sailors' arrival back to land, for their journey has been long. As she sits upon the rocks holding a red pomegranate filled with promise, she sings a song of welcome and consolation for their journey away from the land. As the mermaid sings, her focus shifts from the sailors to the fruit in her hand. Her appreciation of the bounty of mother earth is what gives her heart purpose. These men have been away on the waters, seeking upon the winds of change, distant from the earth for so long. They have been seeking new lands, new adventures, new conditions for growth, and are now returning to the land of their creation where this fruit is home grown. Laughing joyfully, she raises the juicy pomegranate in her right hand as an offering to the unshaven weary men, reminding them of their roots, the land that they left so long ago. They grumble at her in their thirst for fresh water, forgetting the sweetness of life in their yearning for connection to the springs coming from the mountains. She laughs gaily reminding them that once their thirst has been quenched, sweetness awaits. Lifting her head to the blue skies above where sparkles of effervescent light shimmer, she closes her eyes, then connecting to her breath and inhaling receptively, she begins another song of welcome and connection.

Autumn - The Seed

The Seeds of Life - *The pathway to birthing new consciousness, ideas, creations, destinations..*

The seeds lay on the earth's floor as the winds of change blow the loose soils over them, gradually covering them completely. With the rains in the night, they begin to germinate, growing roots of their own and sprouting green leaves into the sunlight. Little seedlings burgeoning here and there, wherever they can. Two little leaves become four, and this life-form forever stretching itself upwards towards the heavens, the roots anchoring it determinedly.

The sailboat tosses about on the stormy seas, its sails down with the captain seeking a patch of stars in the stormy skies between claps of thunder and downpours of rain. He is seeking direction. With dependable determination he holds the boat steady, experience and masterfulness underpinning his confident attitude. He knows the storm will pass. His crew are practised and all wearing bright yellow weatherproof gear as they work together. Maha the whale spouts a column of water from his blowhole where he swims to the right of the boat, bringing comfort and awareness of his support and presence. Once the morning arrives, the sunlight will assist them to orientate themselves. There is nothing to do but keep everything battened down and maintain position as best as possible, till the light appears.

The captain is a powerful man with deep faith and trust. His men believe in him and work together as a dependable and well trained unit. Everyone on the boat keeps an eye on the skies for a break in the clouds, so that they might find compass. Time passes slowly, the rolling waves breaths of mother earth's upheaval, as she rebalances herself with the storm.

Finally, a gradual shift is felt and light lifts a veil on the distant horizon. The waves begin to subside and the pained wind gradually silences. There is a collective sigh of relief amongst the crew as they respectfully lift the sails to a measure, and the boat begins to proceed forward once more.

The earth is sodden with muddy puddles of water everywhere waiting for the sun to arrive and absorb them. Little green leaves appear in the pools, ever hopeful and resilient. New little sprouts of green growing next to fallen old trees who were once upon a time mighty in their presence. Trees whose bodies can no longer withstand yet another storm. They acquiesce, exhausted.

Surrendered to the earth once more, they return home providing protection for new life to grow around them. Slowly those trees disintegrate into the soils, becoming the life giving force and wisdom that the new growth can nourish itself from. Seeds of a new generation.

3

Animals

As the book continues, so does the interdimensional reality of writing each story. You will start to notice the tenses change, the structure of the writing takes on the "I" presence and characters from different stories start to overlap. This is the development of our multi-dimensional nature.

Earth

Reptilian wisdom

Above the earth a white butterfly pure and innocent, flutters freely under a clear blue sky, flying upon unseen designs and patterns of creation.

Upon the surface of the earth the reptilian design can be seen. The design that knows survival within a harsh environment and also contains the serpent energy or life force.

It slithers on its belly with golden yellow eyes and a slitted iris, knowing the doorways between the dimensions. It is free in this respect.

Serpents bring books of knowledge from many places, containing methods of survival and existence. Their forward motion of oscillating West to East, completion and new beginnings of the sunset and sunrise, enables constant progress towards a given destination.

The heart of the serpent is focused and attentive. It moves with wisdom and clarity towards its target, quietly manoeuvring around obstacles. The skin of the serpent sheds when becoming restrictive, and with expansion and growth, the experience of a new sense of freedom arrives. It has the inherent capacity to free itself from the old and limited.

The serpent can ascend a tree moving both vertically as well as in circular motions, enabling a change in perspective with height. They are also able to swim in water very comfortably. A dark serpent in a muddy, choppy river will find its way using smell and intuition. It has a deep inner knowing.

Serpents blend with their environment for protection, and live in alignment with their surroundings which are normally similar to their own in design and colour. The sensitivity of their belly is connected and aligned with the earth herself, constantly receiving messages from their surroundings. Every sound, texture, smell and movement is a message and alert. The frequencies of the earth are as one with them, herself, the script of their survival. When she slows down, so do they. Their eggs of procreation are born unto her their heartbeat one from the moment of conception.

The patterns on their skin reflect the wisdom of their spirit. Some are large with clear designs whilst others appear monotoned and simply textured. Each is unique with their gifts from the Creator, all coming from castles in the sky.

The Crocodile - *the nature of the reptilian part of the brain*

The crocodile lives in the flow of the murky brown river, its body submerged and head above the surface, with ever watchful eyes. He calmly observes life around him, looking for opportunities upon which to feed. His belly is soft and white, his back hard and resilient with a rooftop of scales. He is both vulnerable and a survivor. His tail is powerful and can propel him out of the water and onto the land in an unseen flash attack, paralysing an oblivious victim in an instant. He patiently waits and watches the world surrounding him, missing nothing.

A crocodile stood on the sandy embankment in front of the river watching the swiftly flowing waters pass by. The river was muddy with swells. There was a large cliff behind him where he normally hid in the shadows. The strength of the current was powerful, clearing the pathway before it, and he kept a safe distance from the edge of the current, preferring to observe it rather than to be a part of the anxious surge.

Within the pupil of his black eye evidence could be seen of his connection to the clear night sky. Within the empty dark spaces in-between the sparkles of light, a carriage stood waiting, ready to depart toward far away destinations. The river would carry him to a new life far away from this place. Once in the waters it would be difficult to exit until the river had broken its banks and broadened its width, diminishing to a slower pace. Entering such swift flowing waters could be an opportunity as within the murky depths one could hunt large fish. He hesitated though, for he also knew that there might be larger, faster energies than himself, and he may only be capable of focusing on containing himself within the central stream of the river.

He watched and he waited, gradually merging with its energy and speed, and then entering at a run he tossed himself wildly into it. The edge was bumpy and so he focused on dropping deeper and aligning himself with its more constant centre. Here he could observe his surroundings more easily and be steady in the passage.

Once in the centre of the river and holding himself steady at the bottom, everything became quiet and felt slower. It was an effort to hold himself straight and maintain an awareness for potential obstacles that may be in his path. He sustained his focus breathing slowly and listening carefully for shifts in vibration or temperature. Warmth would mean the river was broadening and becoming shallow and he would be able to exit more easily, possibly onto a large flat plain of earth.

Slowly the temperature rose and he came up for air and visual confirmation. Edging himself cautiously towards the land, he exited the waters into the new unknown territories, feeling vulnerable and exposed. He quickly sought the cover of some brush crawling safely under it for protection, especially from large birds of prey. Breathing heavily he rested a while, becoming accustomed to this new flat terrain with no rocks or cliffs to camouflage himself within. There was only sand and dry vegetation, with open skies above. He acknowledged that the river was the safest place for him to return to, it was shallow and warm, perhaps too warm for comfort, but he could submerge himself safely there. It was moving slowly now and he would have to help himself if he wanted to travel further downstream to seek protective cliffs with shade and cool deep waters. This would provide a more comfortable environment for his nature. He loved reeds to hide in too, places he could conceal himself and emerge from, well fed.

He entered the flow of the river once more, trusting himself to find an environment within which he would feel comfortable and safe, where he would take the time to adapt and live well. The place he discovered had a cliff behind it with many rocks and morning shade. He could watch life at the river from afar, and when the river was low it was a distance from the cliff face with scattered rocks between. He loved this, as life along the river was plentiful and much activity existed here. He also knew that it was the nature of the river to flood from time to time, clearing the debris and expanding its pathway with force. He would stay in this environment for as long as it suited him and then return to the flow of the river when the time was right, to move towards new scenery once more.

His heart felt content and trusting.

The Hippo *- emotional stability, instability in the physical body, as taught by my teacher*

Seeking a higher perspective upon the earth-plane, a giraffe peers out over the African landscape. In the distance he sees a village where an old African man sits to the left of the entrance of his round mud hut.

His stool is carved wood with three spiralling curves supporting two solid round, flat pieces on top. He is chewing on a piece of grass thoughtfully.

He tells me the story of the nature of the hippo who loves to be supported by the water, floating happily day in and day out. However, when walking upon the earth he charges victims spontaneously, a grave threat to many with his heavy weight and focus. It is important, the old African man reminds me, to stay in my emotional body, stay in the water where you are happy and supported floating your days away. He warns me of my aggression when grounded, and my tendency to see much of life around me as a potential threat. He laughs heartily, saying that many fear the hippo the most of all the animals in Africa, especially because it charges unexpectedly in the dark, and is unpredictable. He presses his right index finger on my heart saying, 'Your heart is good but your actions are threatening, be aware of who you are and save your energy for real concerns.'

I see myself as a child, with my red hair in two buns on the top sides of my head and a face full of freckles. I feel unheard and silenced. This feeling of suffocation in my heart. I feel that I must keep the peace and contain my feelings. Over time I become depressed. With all of my emotions all over the place now in my later years, I am alert to danger and prepared to charge. Combined with my issues around trust, my heart is volatile. I need to control my emotional body, learn patience and quiet-listening. I am aware that many times I have no judgement of character simply believing the best in people to my detriment, which once again reaffirms my issues around trust.

I see the hippo running down a long dusty road, the golden sunset before him, his end of day having arrived.

I thank my heart for this deeper understanding of my nature on the earth plane, and the free will to let go of that which no longer serves me, returning myself to balance.

The Goat - *trusting our capacity to achieve a higher perspective*

*Note how the storyteller embodies the archetype and becomes 'I', in the story.

The goat stood at the bottom of the mountains amidst green luminescence. Her horns spiralled over and under in symmetrical connection, spirals of perfect balance on either side of her brain.

Her vision was from a higher plane of existence.

The winds blew erratically across the tops of the mountains shifting clouds and mists, whilst stormy grey skies prevailed above.

She chewed thoughtfully upon a fragrant herb. Its medicine held messages of pathways within. Stories of evolution and keys to her surroundings and environment. She breathed in its fragrance, her lungs absorbing the waves of scent. Suddenly a framed door appeared to her in the night sky. The door was randomly standing in the middle of empty space between the stars.

Directing my gaze deeper into space, I turned the knob and stepped through the doorway. At first there was nothing, I was simply stepping onto the other side of an open door frame in an empty space within the middle of the universe. Looking down I saw some grass and noted that my feet were bare. I became aware that I had a golden crown on my head and wore a white dress. I was sixteen years old. Rolling green hills stretched in every direction under a clear night sky. I removed my crown and placed it on the grass on my right side, as I sat down. I inhaled the crystal clear air and expanded myself into the silence. Presence.

The goat inspected the sharp ascent of the mountain before her, navigating a pathway in her mind's eye towards the top. It was her nature to climb such terrain rather effortlessly, so that she could peruse the landscapes below her from the top of the mountain. From where she stood at the foot of the mountain the grass appeared green and a little wet and slippery, with scattered rocks emerging from the mountainside. Placing her right foot forwards she began her ascent, her heart sure-footed and steady in its beat. Soon she would watch the sun setting to the West and then surrender to the patterns of the starry night sky, receiving their lightwaves of perfection, whilst awaiting the dawning of a new day.

The Lion - *our self empowered nature*

The male lion shook his generous mane as he lay in the shade of the umbrella tree under a hot African sun. He was waiting for this day to cool and the arrival of the golden hour of dusk.

This would be the time when the lioness would hunt and kill fresh meat for him which was a pleasing thought as he observed his amplifying hunger. There was a brief moment of impatience and then he relaxed himself, his ever watchful gaze upon the distant horizon.

Lifting his head slightly he detected the scent of a young impala wafting enticingly upon the breeze. This caused him a deep grunt of dissatisfaction, annoyance at its teasing nature.

He settled himself into the knowing and awareness of his power, including his will over the lioness who served his needs; as was her nature.

The King of the Wild with his rumbling roar, the voice and heart of authority.

Raising his head once again he inhaled the tantalising scent upon the air, his nose twitching at the fresh fragrance.

And then shaking his heavy mane, he stood up and moved himself to the shade of a new location, laying down to doze whilst casting an ever percipient ear to the occasional twitter of the birds in the tree above him.

King of the Jungle - *our multidimensional empowered nature*

A male lion with his proud mane lay in the dusty shade of a tree, on a warm afternoon. He grunted his presence. It was a voice of arrival, a voice of knowing and being. Then laying onto his side his head heavy upon the earth, he closed his eyes and fell into his wild heart; it beat the steady thud and reassurance of his life in this place. He dreamed of a place far, far away with rolling green hills, lush vegetation and the sweet scent of flowers in the air. Where he had the higher perspective of the giraffe and could hide under the ground like a warthog. He became the eagle soaring high with the winds upon his face and firm support beneath his wings. Where he could see the meandering muddy river below, snaking its way across the lands. The lion's breath became shallow as he gazed through the eyes of the eagle at the wild landscape beyond, aware of the blue skies above and the crystalline patterns under his wings. He saw a lake in the distance with still waters reflecting the heavens above, filled with white lotus flowers, pure and magical. A red ladybug rested upon a white petal, inhaling the petals scent and appreciating its soft velvety texture.

The lion yawned, letting out a long breath of acceptance at all of these experiences in his heart. No reason, just here, now. A light breeze rustled his mane bringing his awareness back into his body, his flight complete. He sat upright blinking to his surroundings and perspective. Then, he got up and ambled across the hot earth to seek cooler shade near to the river. He inhaled the scent of the african earth whilst listening to the sounds of the insects buzzing.

The Tiger - *courage and power*

The courage of the tiger with its black stripes, golden-orange and white fur. He is a large, well fed and fearless creature. With four paws firmly upon the earth he saunters into the forest, lifting his head expectantly for a whiff of potential.

His heartbeat is steady, united with the rhythm of the earth and connected to the trees.

He is constantly aware of the air and his breath merged into one, as he studies the frequencies of light around himself with each intended inhalation. His power lies within the awareness of his breath and his connection to his environment. This connection is united with his heart. Thus, he moves himself forwards steadily, unfaltering.

Upon his body each hair, with its particular colour and sensitivity to the light, is attached to the nerves in his flesh. His earthly body is constantly receiving and transmitting awareness with life surrounding him.

His heart pumps courage and strength, continually driving him further into the depths of the forest. And within the depths of the shadows he is connected to the trees and their ability to receive sunlight at the top of the forest. This lightness is inhaled within every conscious in-breath and received by his heart, propelling a deep trust in his progress forwards. He listens attentively to clues within the frequencies, signs within the undulating waves of the air, within the fragrance of the light.

His heart knows that his strength depends upon his awareness of his environment and his connection to it. That his environment is filled with infinite opportunities and options where he can firmly ascertain which pathway appears clearest.

He peered down the trail stretching before him with no end in sight, and his heart trusted his intuition. He saw the clear space between the trees.

Cocking his head to the side, he listened carefully to the stories of the birds in the trees above the trail, and then gently placing his right paw forwards he stepped onto the sandy earth, his senses fully awake.

The Sheep *- ignorance, choosing to ignore*

A single white fluffy cloud floated in a clear blue sky.

A lone sheep on a green grassy hill chewed ceaselessly on the endlessly rooted, rising green blades of grass. With his tummy full and the warm sun upon his back, he held in his heart the comfort of the simple green undulating hills in every direction. The same experience day in, day out.

To the East, stood a lone tree on the hillside patiently receiving the same warm sunlight and breathing in the same imperceptible air. The tree's shadow slowly lengthened down the hill.

With the consistent movement of the sheep ambling around the hill, there was a busyness to the still-life of the picture.

Lost in his world of smells, insect sounds and vibrating growth from beneath him, he raised his head briefly from time to time to peruse his existence in wonder and acceptance. Then after baring his teeth at absolutely nothing, he lowered his head once again and continued to chew noisily.

A man in a dark suit with an umbrella for a walking stick appeared, to idly stroll over the green landscape towards the sheep. His umbrella was evidence of his untrusting nature, what with the presence of one simple solitary cloud overhead.

He halted in front of the sheep and in a nonchalant manner questioned the whereabouts of his missing horse. Without looking up, the sheep stated that he had no idea, never questioning the attire of the so-called rider. And then with his head still bowed down, he continued to focus on the green, green grass, making sure to mind his own business.

On the hill to the East balanced upon a branch, high up in the lone tree, a lark began to sing the song of its heart.

The Chameleon - *merging*

The chameleon is attached to the Tree of Life and energetically blends with its environment. It unites in order to protect itself from potential predators, merging itself with the nature of its habitat.

Its eyes swivel in all directions, all seeing and aware. For it is connected to all that surrounds it. Grids upon grids of overlapping and interweaving layers. The chameleon is both singular and unified.

Seeing is not enough, it needs to **feel** any presence of threat, any potentially unwanted intrusion. To become aware of the finest frequency that emanates with the intent to destroy. The subtle manoeuvring between vision and feeling is a practice that it has mastered for its survival, in order to preserve the gifts its presence holds.

Shifting himself into his feeling body he becomes aware of his physical body's response to its environment. His nerves are alert, prickly and pure, sifting through the layered grids searching for ripples in the waters. And within the swell of each colour's intent, he feels either a surge of delight, or a tale of caution. His mastery is the density of colour, deeply knowing the meaning within each. His body is the mirror. His tongue, long and quick with pinpoint accuracy.

With life around him flowing down his central spine, the nerves read each frequency as a book and he stays within the eternal story of presence. And in this presence of connection, his response is in colour. The fine nerves in his spine appear as fingers of seaweed waving in the ocean, seeking the unseen colours of temperature. The subtle temperatures of the varying colours transmitting clues.

The chameleon, attached to the Tree of Life. Naturally concealed.

The Tortoise - *earthly wisdom and protection*

The tortoise walked slowly across the shrub filled, dry desert landscape. His destination was in his heart and he was determined. On his back his shell contained the patterns of mighty earth wisdom, including the design of the warrior for the earth herself. He exuded from his energy field these designs of perfection, and with his slow and steady tread, from afar, he appeared as a forcefield.

The sun was setting before him and he welcomed the oncoming night with its surrounding spiralling universe, a reflection of the earth's ongoing story.

Pausing for a brief moment he chewed on a few pieces of juicy grasses, receiving their sustenance instantly. Then he pondered upon the completion of the long hot day that had just passed, returning to gratitude in his heart for the earth's nourishment so sweet and tasty. A true reflection of her nature. He loved her so very much.

With the top of the golden ball disappearing into the horizon, the night sounds emerged spilling their voices over the sparse landscape. And within this busy chatter he felt an eternal silence, a perfect balance between earth and sky.

He focused on receiving the patterned light of the stars, the great love from afar. And he listened closely to the sound of his heart gently beating in unison with the earth, a oneness of being. Then he restarted his journey forwards, knowing that his final destination could only be reached with the perseverance of one step at a time.

In the distance was the hazy nighttime outline of blue mountains and trees, where there was the promise of birds, streams and wildlife. A landscape containing the abundant expression of creation, where under a potentially blue sky, many golden-yellow butterflies fluttered freely from flower to flower. He could smell this contrasting landscape, and it excited him. A world filled with joyful activity and creative expression.

Before the dawning of the new day he would arrive, and lap the dew off the soft green foliage, and then rest in the shade of a large tree. He would listen to the whisperings of the secrets that were carried upon the winds. While an eagle flew high above.

The Rhino - *aggressive defensiveness and defensive aggression*

The black rhino is ever watchful, chewing on the leaves from a nearby tree whilst staring at his subject intently. He is simply waiting for a reason to charge. His focus is to understand his subject's protection, that he might destroy it and unwittingly expose any vulnerability. He is always mindful of his physical size and strength, as well as to the presence of his aggressive nature.

Always defending himself. Aggression his game.

He is constantly chewing on something, mulling over the flavours. No matter the Angel wings upon his back, his weight keeps him grounded. The heaviness of his expectations weigh him down. He loves being earthed and has no need to fly or swim. With his nearsighted vision he watches intently, waiting for a reason to charge; to destroy and to trample. His horn can toss victims into a deadly arc, and his aggression and lumbering speed is a wrathful force. Making all that know him alert and respectful to his presence, to his nature.

The Caterpillar - *transforming and embodying higher aspects of consciousness*

A large tree with a white body of bark and a top of swaying green leaves stands firmly in the foreground, with a forest of life bustling behind it.

A little green caterpillar crawled along one of the high branches of the tree towards a succulent green leaf, absorbing light. The caterpillar munched on the leaf until she was completely engorged with the photosynthetic green material, and then retreated to an area between the branches to build a golden cocoon of protection. Once the threads of golden light had been intricately woven into a protective cocoon around herself, she relaxed into the deep knowing of dissolving that which she was into a liquid state, to be reborn and re-patterned with the wings of her ancestors.

A gentle smile manifested upon her lips for this destined moment of change, that was a natural part of her evolution. This was the moment that her heart had been waiting for and her body preparing. It had taken effort and focus to wrap those golden threads of light around her, cocooning her into a space of safety. Now she could totally relax and surrender to her evolution. As she lay there in the breath, slowly dissolving all that she was, she released all of her stories admitting to herself that many of those stories consisted of over identification. There were encounters of the past, moments of fear and anguish, struggle and achievement, times where she had ingested incorrect material, nauseating her and giving her remorse. And then of course, the long journey from the dark interior of the forest to the edge in the light, where her body was able to produce the golden threads of protection for her metamorphosis.

Her ancestors were always present, fluttering around the forest, affirming and encouraging her to continue forwards on her journey towards her destiny. Upon their wings were golden symbols inscribed with blessings that were ever shifting within the still winds of time.

She breathed slowly letting go of all that she was, all she had imagined herself to be and entered a place of absolute surrender. A place where there was nothing, only stillness and a dark sky filled with stars; the light of her creation that had materialised the threads of her cocoon. And then she waited.

From between the stars arrived six white horses with a white carriage. There was a driver in the front with a long whip in his right hand that he used to ignite the air above the horses with a crack. The horses had travelled fast and far, bringing with them a woman inside the carriage of great status and nobility. She gracefully exited the carriage and stood in the empty openness, holding a rolled cigarette at the end of a long filter in her left hand. She spoke respectfully to the spirit of the tobacco appreciating his powerful gifts of connection. Visible patterns in the smoke had assisted her travel.

Her elegant outfit included a white shapely dress, dark pumps and a small black hat on the right side of her head, attached to a little veil. Her eyes were dark and twinkly and she had an air of great charm. She exuded confidence and deep knowing. Her arena of expertise lay in travelling the night skies, the hidden pathways and tunnels between the timelines and dimensions.

She re-entered the white ornate carriage, sitting at the window she peered into what had now become a clear blue sky -the heavens of this plane of existence. She felt into the magnificence of the space around her, experiencing true freedom in its purest untouched form.

Breathing in deeply, and bringing her hands together in front of her heart, she said a prayer of enormous gratitude to her Creator for this place, and for her journey and arrival. She saw him in her mind's eye, eternity in his eyes with a twinkle of delight reflecting like a star. She felt a surge of infinite love for him and for what he had given her the chance to experience. For within the grids upon grids of evolving consciousness, within the circles and cycles of direction, she held the privilege of having encountered the greatest ride of her life.

Opening her eyes, she inhaled deeply, and then in her human form, descended from the skies and entered into the consciousness of the liquid within the golden Chrysalis.

Whilst a magnificent large blue winged morpho flapped his wings near the side of the cocoon, overseeing the progress of his lineage.

Water

The Whale - *deep emotional wisdom and universal knowledge*

A dark grey expanse of water extends to a distant horizon where muted tones of dense clouds are visible. The ripples on the top of the water form peaks of translucent, crystalline clarity.

Deep within the ocean in the dark depths of the unseen, where shifting currents can be felt and echoes abound, glides a black and white whale. Slowly, gently she rises into the light that is streaming through the water, and then breaks through the water's surface. Blowing liquid out of her blowhole, she draws a deep breath of fresh clean air and reveals the joy in her clear brown eyes.

She has been traversing the underworld of dim, murky waters, sludgy and dank, and it has been a disciplined effort. Whilst in that space she perpetually recalls the fresh air far above her, and the warm caress of the sunlight upon her body. These memories propel her onwards, forwards into the ever thickening effluvia. Until finally, there is no farther way into the dense, rubbery resistance and it is time to return. Slowly circling to the right she begins her pathway back. The trail is familiar with diminishing density and ever increasing lightness.

When peering into her brown understanding left eye, the reflection of the stars can be seen in its small black centre. There is also a reflection of pine trees with dark green needles mirrored into her earthy almond coloured iris.

Her large body floats on the surface of the water. Its dark colour is a solid presence in the soft liquid with diamond sunlight glinting off of her back. And the gentle steady beat of her heart responds to the warm air, with a knowing appreciation of being between the two worlds. She is both above and below. In the darkest depths and the purist light.

Breaching Whale - *acceptance in the emotional body, gaining perspective*

The whale effortlessly rises above the dense water into the exalted air. He draws in a deep breath of light and freedom, releasing all effort. For this moment in space has finally been reached after a long and relentless climb. With this moment of complete liberation he then flops back into the water, surrendering into that which carries his substance, that which supports his flow. Oh, to rise beyond the dense surroundings of the normal. To ascend into the lightness of space where the cool air dries surfaces, and time stands still.

He arrives with a gasp of remembrance, inhaling the lightness after the effort of the journey. He has travelled from the dark depths of the oceans bed, rising higher and higher, becoming lighter and lighter, to suddenly break free of the liquid currents. Free from the ever circling sphere of constantly shifting form.

He arrives in that endless moment of poise, within the motionless divide. Where all of existence around and inside, is everything that is and ever has been. Still eternity as it is...in a moment of pause and observation...without breath.

And then, ...to re-engage. He comes back into the body with awareness of the fresh air upon his skin, slowly descending into the liquid wash which creates bubbles of transition. He is relaxed, relapsed into the waves and pathways of co-creation. This returning to the waters, the home of his body so familiar and welcoming.

It is a return to the grids of light and song. It is a harmonious merging into the frequencies of the voice of the creator. It is the connected tale of Great Love.

Going nowhere, simply following the song-lines. This connection to existence is his expression of Being. He moves forward through the criss-cross, ever seeking the essence of the founding frequency, aligning his heart to an undulating thread of golden light, and following its story. A story that unveils connection and expansion.

Dolphin - *emotional wisdom and support*

A dolphin arced joyfully across the silvery stream of moonlight to once again re-enter the ocean's silky interior.

Her eyes were earthy intelligence, and the arc of her movement in the air was the same curve that she undulated along within the waters.

She voiced her recognition and greeting. She was seeing and being seen. The shape of her body lent itself to the curves of the circles and cycles of time. She would effortlessly swim in ascending spirals of connection, until she reached the surface of the water, where she exited. To inhale the lightness of being released into the majestic blue heavens.

The pressure of the water upon her, whilst a form of support, also created influence upon her body. She loved to free herself by ascending into the air above.

She accepted that this was her home, these curved lines of connection. Undulating horizontal threads of light which she swam upon, singing her holy songs of truth.

Her heavy heart felt the pressure of the waters, the weight of the ocean and her knowing of travel along the lines ahead. Always going forward into what felt like the infinite known unknown.

The Crab - *an open heart, stillness and motion. Running between different feelings.*

The yellow petals of a blooming flower lay still, close to the desert floor. It is hardy and resilient to its surroundings. Its furry black interior bristles in the heat, absorbing the light into its spiky centre. The bristles appear as crablike hardy claws extending into space, structured and waiting.

The crab hustles back and forth on the sandy beach between the breaking and dissolving ocean waves. Then digging itself into the sand it seeks shelter from the elements. It submerges itself into the warm golden granules collapsing around it.

Its pincers are serrated and resilient, capable of seizing nourishment as well as providing protection. Under the dance of a night sky, it moves swiftly from side to side, traversing the pathways of understanding between the stars. And this dance in the unconscious, is a dance of seeking and observation.

The scuttling crab in constant motion between the recurrent ocean waves. Waves that thin onto the sand to rapidly dissolve. It is an endless hither and thither dance between, with moments of reprieve beneath, where it finds comfort within the warm earth. This constant dance is the very nature of its existence.

The dark furry centre of the yellow petaled flower, still upon the desert floor. Its hard claws absorb the light into its darkness, whilst the soft yellow petals joyfully open to the heavens above. A stark contrast.

The Barnacle - *attachment*

The pale flat ocean merges into a fading sky, where glimmers of a soft pink sunrise edge the horizon. A single seagull crosses the landscape Eastwards.

The sandy beach has a border of white shells on the water's edge where the waves have discarded them. Stark white forms contrasting with the dark textured particles, upon which they rest.

A white sea-shell, empty of its owner, is washed up onto the sand. It is a cast away from the still aquamarine depths, where life colourfully continues.

Beneath the water upon the rocks, life can skilfully grasp and grip. Even whilst the tides move in and out with the currents sometimes flowing in relentless force.

Here, a barnacle clings to a rock, filter feeding itself within the sweeping waters. It has the ability to bond itself to an object with immovable force. This gift of attachment that anchors itself within the most turbulent waters, is the same gift as the bond that is the divine golden light. The light that flows through the waters of the body and descends into the earth. Once this light has united itself with the body and grounded, it becomes immovable.

So open your hearts and let the light flow into and through the body. Let it unite itself with the earth that the earth lightens, warms and glows with life.

As the rainbow wheels spin and become white light, this golden light irradiates creating connection and protection. Both to the individual as well as the collective.

The Starfish - *stillness in the emotional body, resting into the physical body which contains wisdom and protection*

The defensively aggressive white rhino, when returned to the wisdom of the emotional body, becomes a starfish laying on the sands of the ocean floor. A shark, naturally the hunter, swims overhead seeking scent of a certain sort. The starfish remains still and unnoticed in its peaceful, observant state. The pentagram shape of its form, represents protection and balance.

The Turtle - *submerging into the emotional body*

The turtle entered the clear aquamarine water and began to paddle away from the shoreline. She was not fully grown and this was her first solo journey. She focused her vision ahead as far as she could, staring into the crystalline ocean aware that the water was still shallow with only sand beneath her. Wavy crystalline rainbows of light undulated within her vision. She held within her an awareness for potential shadows that might alert her to company. She was excited for this maiden voyage away from the land.

Popping to the surface for some air, she blinked under the bright blue sky, then diving down and paddling once again, she began to forage amongst some kelp and shells. Nibbling on a piece of soft rubbery kelp gave her immense joy, and she took a moment to appreciate the flavours and listen to the sounds of her own crunching.

The blue ocean was a liquid reflection of the ethereal blue sky above, simply being a more dense version. It was the materialised form of the frequencies of a hovering unseen world.

She continued to listen to the satisfying sounds of her chewing and crunching, and then shifted her focus to the flavours once again; followed by the smell of something new; another flavour, something soft and sweet; and all the while listening and receiving life around her. She loved life in the water and she loved life on the land. In the water she felt the flow and connection of her presence amplify. She was travelling along a current, a pattern of existence which held many pleasures upon its path. She simply needed to be aware and seize each moment with her senses.

She circled to the left and paddled towards land. There she could rest from the constant motion of the water under the shade of a large leafy tree. Arriving, she quietly listened to life in the tree. Then surrendering into the rhythm of her breath, she found connection to the many voices and dance of life around her. Closing her eyes, she connected to the heartbeat of the earth beneath her, and then tuned in to the sound of her heart beating together with it.

The Walrus - *deep truth and knowing*

The Walrus lives in a desert of water and ice, below the crystal blue skies. It has ivory tusks and refined hearing very similar to the family of the elephant.

The golden Being of Lord Ganesha clears the pathways amongst the chaos of the collective unconscious. Pathways for the patterns and light of the stars to flow through. He clears the thick effluvia clouding the pathways.

The walrus lives in crystalline ice and water under a flawless blue sky, revealing deep knowing in his eyes. A knowing as deep as the very bottom of the ocean and as high as the boundless skies above. For in the depths of our soul are our highest connections, opening the pathways for the starlight to arrive, the patterns of our unconscious divine blueprint.

The walrus holds the design of truth and knowing, which keeps the heart in faith and trust and inspires the hands to create. And so we welcome this design which connects the crystalline body to the emotional body, for deeper and higher levels of unification.

The Frog - *transformation through emotional understanding and physical experience*

The frog lives between the lands and the waters. It breeds in the water, its frothy eggs clinging together stickily for protection. Soon, the tadpoles emerge swimming to the depths of the pond where they grow. Gradually their forms shift and change, with little legs appearing so that they may be capable of stepping onto the land and experiencing life around the pond. Like the butterfly in the chrysalis, they also have the ability to shift and change their form in water.

As the night sky descends, they sing the song of their creation to each other and all life around them. And then arriving in silence and closing their eyes, they rest into the remembrance of the night sky. The remembrance of the light designs streaming forth onto the earth plane and between each other. And within this silent connection, they swim in the frequencies of light the same way that they swim in the waters, receiving the flow of life and celebrating their part in it.

Air

The Stork *- the promise of new beginnings, after completion*

A stork flew West across the expansive ruffled waters. Its yellow beak glowed in the afternoon sunlight, its white feathered body heavy with life, although light in flight. His focus was on breathing into the beat of his heart which accompanied the rhythmic pressing downwards of his wings. His heart felt heavy and alone, holding onto the farewell of that which he had left behind.

This experience of low flight in space, over endless waters and expansive skies with so much emptiness surrounding him. Within his heart he held the deep knowing of his direction, yet he had no destination in sight. He only knew that he would fly until the dawning of a new day. A day where the golden rays of sunlight would reflect the truth of his heart. They would illuminate that space where he held the distant recollection and inner remembrance, of another way of being. It was a warm and loving place where golden rays unveiled all that needed to be seen.

Below him other storks had stopped to rest upon shallow, intermittent sand banks. They needed reprieve from the weight of their journeys. They needed to let go of where they had come from and their innermost sadness. With deep breaths and trusting surrender, they gave themselves time to untie from the past, so that they might find the strength for flight once more.

As he flew above them progressing onwards, he sent them blessings and love. He took a moment to acknowledge his own journey, with deep appreciation for the suffering that he had endured like those below him. Then, summoning courage and faith to hold himself airborne, he pressed onwards with perseverance towards the setting sun.

The Moth - *that which is self destructive in nature always seeking light outside of itself*

The moth attaches itself to a piece of organic material gnawing a hole into the intact mass. It is oblivious to the unbroken structure of the material, and only sees the opportunity to feed. Although the fabric is dry in its mouth and much saliva is needed to ingest it, it continues to feed upon it, for this is its nature.

The moth's dusty wings have eyes patterned into their backs, providing protection. Large orbs to scare away potential predators whilst they are busy hollowing out the fabric. Their wings contain layers of particles connected to their surroundings, each particle a receptor that enables it to read its environment. The eyes patterned into their wings sense oncoming danger enabling quick flight in order to hide. Although their eyes appear large and awake, this is misleading to any onlooker. They will flutter away rapidly at the slightest sense of intrusion.

The moth is drawn to the flame of a candle insistently, inviting self destruction. For it has an endless need for warmth and light, outside of itself.

Take note of the design of the moth's nature, for many hold these traits. Those that perpetually seek outside of themselves for brightness to enjoy. It is in their nature to gnaw the grids of materialised form, with an insatiable appetite and a plaguing emptiness. For within this form, there exists a space of darkness, an emptiness that needs to consume.

The Hummingbird - *seeking the sweetness of life, alone but connected*

The hummingbird seeks sweet nectar from the North. She drinks the elixir of the flower to raise herself into its golden stream of light. She pursues the sweetness of life. Returning to sit on a branch in a tree, she simply breathes and waits whilst listening to the sounds of life around her, and feeling the rustle of air upon her feathers, connected through her breath.

Her heartbeat is rapid. Suddenly she feels herself high in the air in flight, her powerful wings guiding her along the airwaves with pinpoint accuracy. She lands on a neighbouring tree where she watches a black panther with emerald eyes and a well fed body. It is on the prowl, being the curious nature of a cat. Above the greenery of the forest floor flutter white butterflies, freely. She scratches her head intently with sharp claws, trying to remember the spot deep in the forest where the bees have a hive. Keeping still she listens carefully for a possible faint hum over a distance. She hears the bees busily working together to make sweet honey. Although both creatures create from the nectar of the blossom, the hummingbird marvels at how the bees work together in community, creating together from a structure of pure perfection. Each one knows its place and function perfectly. The hive hums with golden designs of love and devotion. Travelling upon translucent wings the individual bees seek the sweetness of life, always returning to the whole. The hive carries the sweetness of many different blossoms. Its scent is a magical stream of inspiration wafting across the landscape and blessing all in its path.

The hummingbird truly appreciates this vision and sound. The beehive's essence reminds her of something that she does not have. As much as she loves the forest with all her friends, she enjoys seeing and appreciating the community of the bees.

Taking flight she heads towards the pond in the East where the white lotus flowers bloom in silence, the still waters of the pond a reflection of the heavens on high. A mirror to an open heart.

The Kingfisher - *pinpoint accuracy when seeking within the emotional body*

The Kingfisher shimmers in iridescent blues in the afternoon sunlight. He has a strikingly unyielding red beak that connects with pinpoint accuracy when entering the waters. This precision is a result of the connection between his heart and the very tip of his beak.

At speed, his eyes close on impact of the water for it is the purpose and intent of his heart's strike that guides his way forward. Nourishment is his intention. He seeks connection between the desired object and its pre-placement within his heart.

He is simply aligning the frequencies and then materialising the outcome.

The unyielding red beak so brightly coloured and clearly seen, leads the way into the waters breaking their reflective surface. Upon arrival beneath, the colour within the water immediately dulls.

With liquid streaming across the surface of his feathered body, his speed is fleeting. He opens his mouth to capture its desire, and then without a sound and simply using momentum, he rotates returning to the skies. Upon exit of the water he cracks open his wings, with his beak holding the nourishment of his heart's determination.

The Butterfly - *trusting our connection with the breath*

The newly freed spirit with delicate wings absorbs the surrounding air. She gently breathes in the frequencies and patterns of light, reading the stories of her environment. Sacred symbols flow through the light into the little nerve endings in her wings. Regenerating the knowing within her spirit of the state of her universe. This connection of the elemental body to its wings, builds intuition and trust in the deep knowing of our surroundings and our universe. It gives us the freedom to stay connected in a heartfelt way. The energy flows into the centre of the back at the higher heart, easing the stresses of the heart. The metamorphosis of the butterfly from an earthbound creature into flight, needs a strengthening of the breath where the wings meet the body. This enables the spirit to feel free and soar, and the heart to feel light.

Throughout the lineage of our ancestors, many have freed themselves before us, to soar above the earth-plane bringing beauty and remembrance, when noticed. Their wisdom is in our blood for they too have walked this path. Sometimes they too walked in stillness and without direction wondering which way to continue. The wind from the East, the sun in front and the ocean to the West.

Within each heart is the beat of freedom, united to a star far away, calling through space and time to be remembered and returned. This spark of our creation is the very light of our existence. This is the light that is in our hearts shining upon the space surrounding us, that we might see the pathway.

The lost spirit roams in the dark night of the desert, sensing prickly cacti and dry sand. So many obstacles to contend with. How to find a way. But the spirit of the white butterfly, pure, innocent and trusting, recognises the symbols in the lightwaves of the day. The messages being written into its wings presenting the story of its universe.

It breathes steadily into that place where the wings meet the body, slowly becoming stronger and stronger into the deep knowing and remembrance of flight. Flight that enables the spirit to roam freely, knowing intuitively where to go. Knowing which flowers wait ahead, summoning with the sweetest fragrance and the brightest colours. The deep knowing of the heart is enough.

The Owl and the Eagle - *wisdom of the heart and higher vision*

The mighty oak stands firm and steady in the forest, light bark and bright green leaves visible in the shadowless night. In the hollow of its heart lives the owl, the wise elder with her wide open bright orange eyes and 360 degree vision into the dark, into the unconscious.

During the daytime, she is sheltered within the comforting dark cave of the tree's heart, aware of life around her. At night, she flies over the shadowy landscapes with a speciality in creatures that slither and snoop. Her wingspan is large and under the light of a rising full moon, she misses nothing. She has discerning vision in the darkness, where unseen intentions and hidden agendas aren't as apparent.

Clucking as she sits on a branch, she feels annoyed at the serpent, who is rather optimistically climbing her tree. He is large and dark and seeks her eggs, to feed upon. The potential new life those eggs hold might sustain his dark nature for quite a while, as well as give him great satisfaction. With intention I remove him from my consciousness, dissolving him into the light. I am the owl and the serpent is the life-force of ill intent. The owl returns to her home in the tree to make sure that her three little eggs containing the life she wants to birth, are still there. Heavenly blue little ovals with brown specks of earthly wisdom, lie trustingly in the nest. Clucking lovingly this time, she warms them with her body and soul.

As she sits in the cave of darkness protected and still, she listens to the winds rustling the leaves in the higher branches of the tree above her, and feels the tingle of awareness that the whispers bring. The breath of life blows through the green little hearts, speaking of places far away, telling stories of change and days to come. The leaves flutter in response to the messages, bending in acknowledgment of the unseen commands.

The owl shuffles her earthy-brown stippled feathers relaxing into the moment of now, aware of the three little developing lives beneath her. She is a natural protector with fearful claws and soaring heights. She willingly drops a writhing threat from a higher plane where detail of the landscape is lost due to an ascended perspective. She readily releases the weight of menace, freeing it from its dark intentions and earthly concerns.

The eagle is similar to the owl. Although his strength is the winding muddy river which connects to the wisdom of the mountains, the landscapes on either side of the river, and its eternal flow towards the ocean.

While the eagle flies primarily during the daytime, the owl enjoys the dark. Both have the gift of higher vision and flight. They use the air beneath their wings to press down upon, for therein lie the many unseen patterns of the divine. Within the black pupil of the eagle's eye is a perfect night sky. The light of the star's designs connect his vision that he might see anything out of the ordinary, any distortions.

The owl's connection to the deeply rooted tree and the divine expression of earth's nature, assists her vision at nighttime, enabling her ability to see that with corrupt intention. For the purity of mother nature's heart is majestic and anything that wishes to interfere or destroy her divinity, is doomed.

The winged ones, those with higher vision and connection to the mountains, the trees, the rivers and the soils. Connection to the flow of life on earth.

Fire

*Dragon - can walk on the **earth**, swim in the **water**, fly in the **air** and breathe **fire**. They have all four elements and are balanced creator beings*

The female dragon was contained in a rectangular room and she was heavily saturated with emotion. Her small wings flapped to gain strength. Her breath of fire was strong but her ability to move her body was slow and cumbersome. Her body was filled with water, swollen and bulging and the effort to walk forwards entailed rolling her body from side to side. She was happy to blast fire from her mouth, randomly.

Closing her eyes she imagined letting the heavy fluid go, breathing it out in hot misty breaths of release. She was aware of the closed room around her, and the ceiling above. In her mind, she placed herself on the top of a green hill under the blue sky and called the sun to evaporate the water that she was consciously breathing out. With every claggy out breath she released more moisture. It was a process of moving the excess liquid from inside the body into the misty breath of release, and then allowing it to evaporate into the warm air. Keeping her eyes closed she inhaled deeply into the centre of her emotional heart, focusing on freeing herself with each out breath.

Gradually she felt herself becoming lighter, and her wings expanding until they could stretch far beyond her body, until she was able to lift herself from the earth and rise above the situation. Humming a song of connection to herself she stretched her consciousness beyond the blue skies into the universe, into the starry night sky. The patterns of light - the design of her creation.

She focused her awareness on her sense of freedom from the earthplane. She saw the open shackles and chains that had been tied around her legs, laying on the earth below. She was free to soar above. Free to sing her songs with the wind beneath her wings, and the warm setting sun upon her face. Her breath was a prayer of gratitude for her ability to hold vision from this height.

As the sun subsided into the horizon, the clouds resting upon the ledge became soft shades of pastels with compassionate pinks. She felt compassion in her heart for her chains of suffering and her attachment to the earthly realm as she reflected upon the completion of the day.

She returned her awareness to her expanded wings supported by the air beneath, as she soared along the unseen patterns in the light.

Her body was a green reflection of mother nature below and her eyes were as black as a starless night sky. Empty and silent. Therein lay the nothingness that had existed from before her journey had begun, before the patterns of the stars were dreamed into being. A time when the potential for the light of existence was everywhere. In that still dark everywhere, lay her hopes and dreams.

She steadfastly held the wide open expanse of her wings in position, cruising upon the layers and levels of designs, unseen to the unseeing eye. Always adjusting her frequencies of acceptance and being, she knew that each plane of perception at any given height brought with it a different understanding and feeling. Slowly descending from on high in great spirals of connection and comprehension, she arrived once again to stand upon the rolling green dusky hills of her heart. In remembrance the starlight above materialised into form around her.

4

Landscapes

The Landscapes of Mother Earth as the Landscapes of our Consciousness

The Wisdom of the Mountains - *our bodies design is connected through the breath to the patterns of our original creation*

Earth/Physical

The rocks that make up the mountains, form at its most dense. The oldest designs of the earth contain the original patterns of creation. The power and strength of these landscapes of our design stand tall and true, immovable under a clear blue sky.

The thoughts that float in our minds beneath the clear blue heavens of freedom will eventually land in the body to run around without direction. When gazing towards the mountains of wisdom both near and far, small and large, they rise from the earth into the skies uniting the horizon in sacred symbols of design. When we stretch our vision towards the farthest reaches of the horizon where heaven meets earth, and where we reach for that place wherein the empty landscape of stillness stretches into the horizon. It is within this space that our Faith and Trust in the design of our creation stays true. Where we can trust in the design of our planet, our teacher, where we stand, connected as One with no separation. It is here in this place that you hold the vision of your wise-hearts dreaming for a life of clear blue skies and stillness. And it is here that you can expand yourself beyond the blue skies of clarity and deepen into a starry night sky, to trust in the blueprint of our creation.

The Cave - *the heart*

Earth/Physical

Within the cool darkness of the cave is a silent still space of nothing and everything, of nowhere and everywhere. It is a place wherein the potential to connect to the experiences of my existence are available. It is within this still empty place that my soul yearns to explore, and my heart willingly opens the door.

I breathe deeply into the roots of my tree feeling the Great Mothers sturdy support and her love entering my heart with each inhalation. My entire body fills with love as I breathe out. I do this for a while and I ask my body what precisely it needs in this now moment, in order to be free. A vision appears of Father waiting silently on his camel in the quiet stillness of the desert, below clear blue skies. I stand before him and his wise camel, squinting up at him with curious wonder. First with his left arm and then with his right he opens and extends his arms and hands towards the horizon, the landscape surrounding us. He instructs me to breathe this stillness in. To breathe in acceptance of all that I am without seeking anything. To simply be.

I close my eyes feeling the freedom of the blue heavens overseeing me from on high, the warmth of the golden sand beneath my bare feet, the slight breeze upon my face reminding me that I am alive and on the Earthplane. And then, with the sun on my back - I will myself into still acceptance - alternating between love through my roots and acceptance of all that I am, and all that is. Slowly my body completely relaxes as the feelings connect into it. I feel my power and see my golden crown on my head, my white feathered wings upon my back, my eagle of protection hovering high, gliding gently in circles and infinity shapes. I feel a deep sense of trust in my heart for this dark unknown yet so very known infinite space of calm. A deep knowing that lifetimes are playing out in consciousness as I breathe, and I am remembering myself. Whatever I need I have the experience of and access to, I simply seek within my heart the answer to my question. Peaceful acceptance. I have all that I need. I am all that I need.

The eagle slowly descends and perches on the left shoulder of Father, squawking his approval. I breathe into the cool dark empty space of the cave, becoming aware of crystals embedded in the cave walls. They are slowly beginning to illuminate and glow. Countless colours with multifaceted patterns illuminating the darkness in soft crystalline clarity. I felt love slowly lighting my heart. Love for the blue skies, the heavens of freedom, love for my deep roots and connection to the various magical landscapes of the Earthplane. I felt love for the wind on my face, the ocean, the mountains and rolling green hills alive with flowers, the forests, the lakes and the deep stillness of the desert.

As my consciousness travelled over these landscapes of my knowing, I remembered my courage to get to know them all. Lifetimes in each one, with experiences to parallel and amplify my connection. I remembered the sweet scent and taste of strawberries, the snow on the mountains, standing under the force of the waterfall and surfing the ocean waves with the dolphins. I remembered seeing vistas of beauty through the eyes of the eagle and inhaling the sweet aroma of delicate petals, being a queen in a castle and a beggar on the street, with an empty bowl. And I remembered being the brightly coloured butterfly, free to fly after a long wait of crawling.

I looked at the cave walls and saw many golden inscriptions of sacred symbols, hieroglyphs and numbers. Stories of my creation, my existence in time and space within these planes. And I sighed a breath of release. I am here. All is well.

The Desert - *emptiness, abandonment, neglect, abuse, interference from chemicals or by unethical beings. The deserted landscape.*

Earth/Physical

The inexorable desert - a sweeping stretch of undulating sandy hills. Patterns of the wind etched into a moment, under pressing blue skies.

Within the ripples of the sand written into patterns of design, lay the stories of consciousness within this plane of existence. A book for the reading. The entire library of this Now Moment.

And if one should peer beneath the uppermost layers of movable sand, there is a more solidly embodied story of before. Layers and layers rest upon the founding formations of solid creation; sacred symbols in stories, underpinning the ever shifting particles.

The sand blows this way then that way, travelling from one distant direction across to the other. And in between are moments of stillness baking under a relentless sun, a fiery ball trailing across a still blue sky.

Without warning, a whisper of wind becomes a roar of blinding dust, blocking any vision or recall of what may have once been or what might yet arrive. And within this mindless chaos whilst struggling to stay upright and move forwards, we take one carefully controlled step in front of the other, pondering direction.

I sit in the shadows of a hill in the dark, breathing particles of fine dust swirls, deepening into the centre of my heart, knowing that this too shall pass. All of this superficial surface disturbance is transient, whilst my roots are connected to the library below - The Book of Earth. Her sacred designs are the very foundation of my Being. I feel my ever deepening roots stretching downwards seeking the divine virgin. I feel my resilience increasing and myself becoming steadier as I grasp a foothold.

My spirit arrives with Angels wings. My heart expands, her beat steady. I am committed to walking through the landscape of this plane of existence.

The River - *connection to the different landscapes*

Water/Emotion

The afternoon sun glints off the top of the river, creating sparkles of diamond light in celebration. Twinkles bounce up and down whilst the river flows relentlessly beneath. This time of the day, each moment after the other, and before the next; is captured within the heart and held with precious intent. For the river flows from the wisdom of the mountains to the collection of the sea, connecting all along its path.

The river of life, the flow of existence is what connects us to the different landscapes of the earth-plane and the different dimensions of ourselves. As the eagle flies over the winding river, our vision becomes clearer. A higher perspective on the flow and connection of our lives becomes visible, as we weave between the mountains of wisdom and the planes of change. Within each of our diamond hearts is the clarity of all that we are; a pure, resilient and crystal clear soul.

However, just as some rivers are brown and the water unclear, so too are there lives that we carry that are burdened with the weight of mud. Lives containing a lack of clarity and under-standing of that which we have learned from them.

This may be represented as energetic blocks within our bod-ies in the physical form of adipose tissue.We literally carry the weight of these burdens on the physical plane, here now. Diet and exercise may clear these blocks, however, with many life-times of distortions some of these patterns have materialised and the blocked flow of the body has become slow and heavy.

Within each of our unique hearts is a truth of the flow of our individual light, and also that which we resist. With a higher perspective of the workings of our true nature, we are empowered to unblock and clear that which no longer serves us.

How am I able to do this? Come into your heart with greeting, 'Hello my heart, I Am here, and I hear the voice that cries for a clearer understanding of my soul's pure light'.

Within the muddy river are many fish that suffer and cannot breathe properly, for there are particles of sand that pass through their lungs and disturb their soft inner flesh. But they have no choice, for this is the river that they were born into and it is all that they know. However, should we get the flow of the water just right, the flow of the emotional body carefully balanced, these particles of sand will have time to descend onto the bed of the river, and the waters will become clearer and more crystalline. Our suffering will become less and we will have more clarity. When the river flows rapidly our emotions rise, and the sand lifts from the bed of the river. The intensity of the flow feels uncontrollable and uncomfortable. We experience ourselves as the suffering of the fish.

So begin by coming into the heart and listening to the flow of reason, trust and self knowledge.

"Hello my heart, I Am here, I embrace all that I Am, acknowledging and appreciating all of my suffering. I wish to open myself to the light of my soul and to remember the wisdom of all that I have learned. I wish to let go of my pain, my suffering, my torment and return to peace and tranquillity. Within my heart is the prayer of my soul to love myself and all that I AM, understanding that my choices have taught me so much of the flow of the river. Much is hidden in the muddy river that I cannot see, but I feel it in my heart and I know that these disturbing feelings hold much wisdom. Wisdom that will influence the choices that are in my path before me. I trust these feelings, for I know that the suffering of the past holds the wisdom to guide me with the choices on the path ahead, beckoning me into the light."

A little bird tweets whilst flying over the river, singing greetings and gratitude for the flow of life that the river is. Our spirit, singing appreciation for that which we are willing to release, so that the flow can become more gentle and that we can experience calm once again.

Let Spirit lift the burdens, the weight off of our shoulders, that we can spread our wings and open our hearts and feel a sense of freedom. That we can trust in the flow of life and that which we are co-creating. As One with all life.

The Eagle and the River - *higher perspective and deeper understanding*

Air/Mind & Water/Emotion

The eagle flies high in a clear blue sky with the wind beneath his wings, gliding along the unseen pathways and patterns within the boundless blue space. He looks upon the picture below at the unfolding story taking place on either side of the river.

To the West the sun was setting, and to the East the sun was rising, with the constant flow of the river winding between. A serpent flow of life, with its own beginning and end.

Within this clear flow of water, unseen to the human eye, are serpent designs of creation in divine patterns of perfection. Designs revealing the wisdom of the earth below, and upon its surface reflections of the heavens above.

This appeared to the eagle as layer upon layer of patterns in varying depths and transparencies, each a reflection of the truth of connection. Connection from the wisdom of the mountains through to the vast depths and ever shifting tides of the ocean.

The eagle studied the river carefully, seeking within the layered patterned reflections a clue to the unfolding story, the story of the earth and her evolution. The rising state of her condition, her story. He noticed the thinning dark lines that were holding the patterns in place, the way that they were fading in and out within the layers and levels. A gentle merging was happening between the layers. The overlays exquisitely blending with those beneath, creating swirls within the lines. This was the uniting of the soft and gentle nature of creation, with firm structure. And within this blending of flow, a clear message could be read in the shimmering lines and circles rising and falling within the water. A simple voice between the earth and the heavens, coming into form. The flow of the river, the serpent of life and light, holding the symbols of evolution within the clear waters of the divide. The story of the evolution of materialised consciousness within a sphere of light, beneath the wings of the eagle. He studied the depths of the winding river seeking the message his heart yearned to receive, and that only clear waters can unveil. He searched within this merging of space between the blue skies above, and nature below. The inter-weaving fabric of the waters, majestic and powerful. His heart responded with faith and gratitude.

All is well and as it is. This story of evolution and flow. All is well and as it should be.

He circled to the left lowering himself onto a new pattern of design within the clear blue skies. He directed himself home with a deeply appreciative and accepting heart, holding this moment, holding the message as a steady beat in his heart.

The Nature of the River *- the importance of doing yoga and moving flow through the physical body. Staying connected.*

Earth/Physical & Water/Emotional

A serpent river winds across a flat landscape. There is no vegetation on either side of the river, only a dry cracked desolate earth. Above, a burning sun blazes in a clear blue sky and there is simply no moisture in the air. The terrain is empty of life.

A giraffe gazes across the empty landscape and horizon seeking something far away, 'over there'. Whilst 'here' at the water's edge, life could be growing. To tend and create the garden of paradise occurs here at the river's edge, the river that flows between the different landscapes.

One would loosen the earth creating space for the breath of life beneath the soil. It is in this place that the seeds of new creation can breathe and receive light, coming to life. By very gently directing the flow of the water, the seeds are nurtured whilst seeking the light of the sun. This is the nature of their design.

Within each seed is a sprout seeking the light, a sprout that knows that within the light is the pattern of its heart. That its heart will open to receive the love, the light from above and unite with the design of its resonation. Within our DNA these seeds exist waiting for the opportunity to awaken to life and come into expression. We need to loosen the physical body with yoga or exercise, like the soil of the earth, to open the physical vessel that the cells can breathe and receive light. And then by navigating our emotions and directing the water very gently into the physical body, they receive the nourishment that they need. At first the body is hard and resistant, this may feel uncomfortable, perhaps even painful with suffering. However, with our labours of determination and perseverance, the soil becomes loose and the breath of life and light can reach the inner dark spaces once so compacted and hard, that yearn to come to life once again. Eyre caution with the waters, always be aware and conscious of the flow of feelings so as not to drown or wash away the seeds that you have so diligently worked back into life, back into the light.

The power of the water can be a mighty river clearing all in its path and lifting the soil from below creating unclear muddy waters. And this muddy, swiftly flowing river passes through the shadow of the tallest cliff, with almost no reflection on the surface, the dark shade and constant movement making reflection unavailable within that space of time, the ripples on the surface ruffled and the heartbeat so deep within the earth with the flow of the river so quick. Surrender to this place as one with Mother Earth, Mother Nature. For these places exist and are part of our nature, as seen visible on the earth plane. As our light arrives upon the earth, our nature is as one with hers, in alignment with the nature of her being.

Feeling and seeing the ripples on the water in the shade of the cliffside, the muddy brown liquid flowing so belligerently with the force of gravity and surplus. The rainfall seems to arrive from hidden passageways within the mountains and this ever expanding river perilously forcing its seams to breaking point, transporting all along its path with it.

Finally it reaches a plateau, broadening and slowing down to a steady beat under the full sunlight and open landscape. A peaceful stillness prevails with the surrounding open horizon, as the serpent winds its way steadily towards the ever welcoming blue ocean. And in the distance white storks with large yellow beaks are flying North over the dusky seas.

The River to the Ocean - *the importance of drinking water to stay connected to the body's earthly wisdom.*

Water/Emotional & Earth /Physical

There is a place in the heart seen by the eagle, where the river flows into the ocean. The fresh waters from the mountains merge into the salt waters of the sea, and there is a merging of the worlds.

The land in-between the mountains and the sea is primarily salt free except for specific points.

Let us visit one of these salt pans upon the land which exists as a result of evaporation, a place where there is no longer any water. It is a powerful place for the salt crystals will connect themselves to the energy in the area and absorb the many varied frequencies. The human body is the same. When it is dehydrated it absorbs the energies around it, which can sometimes interfere with the soul signature frequencies of the individual, creating feelings of confusion.

Like the salt laying upon the earth near the mountains, the frequencies of the salt synchronise themselves with their environment, affecting the feelings around the heart. Although the light from the sun and the blue heavens above continually bless the crystals, the physical connection to the land on which it lays is its primary connection. Both are connected to the same heartbeat of the earthplane, the same pulse of life. Our master teachers and guides keep clearing our energy fluid, but self empowerment will be the awareness to remember to do it self. With a blessing of the water before drinking it, you may allow it to wash through the body as the river flows across the lands connecting the frequencies of the land to itself and ultimately connection to the ocean, the oneness of Being. Connection to that deep intuitive knowing that one feels through the body, as deep as the ocean. Allowing feelings to flow out of the hands and feet from that which the body is connected to.

For as the ears listen to the universe and some sounds are more heard than others, such is the body - it absorbs the frequencies surrounding it.

Living in an environment close to nature will bring the body into balance, for the frequencies of nature hold the patterns of perfection to which the body yearns to return. The natural salt water within the body always returns balance to the whole.

Within the depths of the ocean are the bottom feeders, and it is their design to clean and clear so that balance can be maintained.

As the rainbow is reflected within the clear particles of water within the air, so does the river hold the patterns of the land it has flowed across, into the ocean. One feels within the body the flow of all life around one, and now with increased levels of awareness to both the seen and unseen worlds. Keeping the bodies flow balanced with clean water is the same as the rivers on the earthplane. What we put in the rivers and our bodies affects the ocean, the feelings we carry as individuals and as a collective.

The Oasis - *support in a deserted landscape*

Water/Emotional & Earth /Physical

Within each of our consciousness we hold in our hands our book of knowledge, with the written keys to unlock our understanding of the pathways we have chosen to experience and learn from.

Through connection to the core of our hearts we are able to access these pathways which may appear to journey into the unknown. We are in essence, following the trails of light home. With focus and a heartfelt destination, we are able to pass by many distractions and opportunities of relating. We choose our course and that which we might learn from it.

With the spark of my creation appearing as a star in the clear night sky before me, I connect into my heart. This star holds the signature frequencies of my soul's light, and my heart is yearning for reconnection and unity, and so I surge forward towards home.

Home appears as an oasis in the desert. A reuniting of friends and family around the calm waters edge under a clear blue sky. The water is transparent and crystalline containing the frequencies of clarity and trust, where everything is visible. Within the waters the movement of luminescent fish can be seen reflecting crystalline patterns of perfection. They emanate geometries of light transmissions into the air above, green-blue pulses of design flowing upwards.

I gaze over the calm reflective waters focusing on its materialised expression. A mirror of the Heavens on high. In the distance I can hear the playful voices of the children and across the water I can see a camel prepared and ready for passage, his back carrying the necessary items for the journey. There are white butterflies surrounding the water's edge where the vegetation grows.

Here exists the wild, pure spirit of freedom.

The dark pupil of the hawk flying overhead, reflects a clear night sky.

The Oasis II - *trusting, despite arid conditions*

I am in the desert upon the earth-plane and there is a vast empty space of blue horizon with a sea of sand surrounding me. The heat burns my feet and my throat is dry with cracked lips. I steadily walk in the direction of an imagined oasis. The dark nights reveal three stars shining their light. They are always in my thoughts, guiding me to what appears as a nativity scene of the birthing of a pure consciousness.

I finally arrive at the Oasis, immediately going towards the water to completely submerge myself into it. The water is warm in the late afternoon sun and it is surrounded by many friendly palm trees. There are children playing, families, friends and animals, all busy, joyful and present.

I once again sink myself below the water into the deep silence of my soul, listening for my heartbeat, steady and true. And then my face breaks the surface of the water into the light, fresh air gently brushing my skin and greeting me to life. I am here now.

The Lake - *opening and respectfully reconnecting to the heart after a long and harrowing journey*

Water/Emotional, earth/physical

The protea flower with its divine patterns of perfection, grows upon the mountain sides in dry conditions. It is capable of surviving the most destructive winds, standing strong and resilient to everything but fire.

Appearing quite similar in design is the Lotus Flower, however this flower grows in water, floating upon a calm lake. It gently bobs up and down, easily affected by the slightest disturbance. Both flowers contain the same divine patterns of existence. However, where the soft, gentle, velvety petals of the lotus flower are easily torn, the protea remains hard and steady in the wildest of winds. Her luminous pink petals glow translucently in the sunlight, spikes seeking the warmth and light from above. Bee's steer clear of the protea's protective petals when entering the inner gifts of sweet juiciness. It takes a courageous bee to find its way into the centre of the protea and drink from her pleasures. Having satiated his thirst for the sweetness of life, he will fly away, disappearing quickly.

Alternatively, the invitingly gentle curve of the delicate petals of the lotus flower resting upon the waters, beckon for all to approach. Under the blue blue skies, the calm of the lake perceptibly responds to the slightest breeze, the slightest suggestion of any motion.

High in the sky, a stork surveys the lake below, searching for a place to land, a place to rest its weary body. With its pure white feathers and golden-yellow beak, it glides smoothly downwards. Then spotting a large, green lotus leaf, it lands skilfully upon it, balancing itself carefully to unite with the motion beneath. It takes a few deep breaths in order to recover from its long flight, then adjusting itself it relaxes into a state of peaceful rest, feeling the welcoming effect of the waters underneath it. The stork's nature is to fly long distances over vast expanses of water to arrive at an exact location. It had found momentary reprieve on this gentle, undisturbed, shallow section of the lake where these glorious flowers with large green leaves grow. The stork looked into the centre of a nearby flower and noticed a bee drinking pleasurably from its juices. Whilst pondering from whence it had journeyed, the bee took flight vanishing into thin air.

The stork swallowed a long cool drink from the water and then inhaled a few more deep, restful breaths. All was well, the waters were peaceful. Swirls would appear at the slightest movement from below, above or upon it.

Peering into the distance she noticed a large serpent gliding towards her through the water. Its undulating body was causing ripples across the surface, resulting in shimmers of diamond glittering light. As the serpent drew nearer, she noticed the diamond patterns on its skin in browns, indigos and purples with an underlying compassionate pink. The serpent arrived with wisdom and love, enquiring of the stork's well-being. The stork looked into her kind loving eyes and understood that she was the guardian of the lake.

'This is a magical place', she said 'so still yet so powerful. The water's expansive response to any disturbance or frequency, and this lily pad that I'm standing upon, so strong yet so easily broken.'

'Yes,' said the serpent of the lake, and began to share her wisdom.

'Be careful with your talons. Always stand respectfully on the surface of the leaf for her roots grow deeply into the earth where she gathers the light messages from the embedded jewels. These leaves then transmit prayers to the heavens for that which the earth is needing. The responding light from above is a blessing to her, and she grounds and roots this light back into the earth, nourishing that beneath her with its love. The winds sometimes damage her, even occasionally breaking her stem away from her roots, disconnecting and separating her from the earth. Soon though, from within the earth, the roots of the lotus flower will push out another green leaf, so that she might continue this message interface. This receiving and transmitting of the light from on high, the love of the high heavens. The deeper her roots grow into the soils the stronger she becomes, and the thicker her leaves develop in the light. Until the dark green communication interface has the subtle expertise of deep knowing. She invites the bees who travel through the dimensions of time, to feed from her wisdom. She allows them to take this sweet deep inner knowing into their sacred patterned homes, where ancient knowledge is held through all lines of time, and can be generously shared with other life on earth. Her sister, the hardy protea is more difficult to approach, and her roots are more shallowly embedded into the earth. She shares her wisdom with the sunbirds with their long beaks, and they understand what they are drinking.

The sweetness of life from a long journey can only be appreciated with a gentle and respectful heart. An open heart that knows the struggle of disconnection. A heart that remembers what it feels like to be the receptor and transmitter of knowledge between the earth and the heavens. A heart that holds the patterns, the juices of sweetness as generous offerings to those around it'.

The serpent looked deeply into the eyes of the stork, with appreciation for the gift of new life that she held. She bestowed upon her blessings for the continuation of her journey, having shared with her some of the wisdom of the lake.

'Come and rest here anytime you need to', she told the stork, 'no matter where your journey is taking you. The wisdom of the lake is magical and you are merely standing upon the surface.'

The stork thanked the serpent and then drawing in a deep breath, she pressed down upon her wings lifting herself gently off the lotus leaf, careful not to cause any damage. Then raising her face towards the East, she continued with her flight.

The Murky Lake - *confronting that which plagues one*

Water/Emotional

The lake was nestled at the bottom of green rolling hills, the sun glinting diamonds off its surface. An otter frolicked playfully in the water, slipping into its depths and popping to the surface for light and air. His whiskers were long and wet, his eyes were clear but with a concerned depth to them. He exited the water to go and sit on the land on a hillside in the shade.

From the top of the hill approached an older man, he had a hat on and a comfortable gait. He sat down on the left side of the otter and enquired of his well being. The otter felt a sense of sadness sweep over him and tears welled up in his eyes. The water of the lake was murky and unclear and he was unable to see in front or below him. He could not see other life in the lake and felt alienated. He had come to this side of the lake to receive an overview and get a feel for what was wrong, and he didn't want to climb too high up the hill, as it felt safer to have near access to the water. He took a long deep breath of fresh air and became still. What could be clouding the clarity of the water on such a clear day? Little particles of slimy brown growth were everywhere making it murky, and he wondered how to clear it.

The brown slippery particles were growing faster and faster and it was becoming darker and darker. Soon the once crystal clear lake would be brown and slimy with growth. He looked to the man on his left and saw a deep knowing in his twinkly blue eyes. The man gazed at the dark hue and lack of clear depth. There was an overgrowth of earth particles with slimy surrounding mucus. And the surface of the water appeared to have a very fine layer of oily colours upon it reflecting the sunlight. They swirled and moved in tantalising patterns and although holding a certain beauty, the reflections were destructive to life underneath. What was creating this filmy layer and how could one remove it?

The man pointed towards the edge of the lake to reveal the problem to the otter, who nodded appreciatively.

At the edge of the lake on a thick stem of grass was a locust, noshing away voraciously. His eyes were segmented and he had multi-dimensional vision. He could see everywhere at once, above, around and below. He was chewing the juices from the grass and then spitting the remains into the water. An oily film spread from the grass, remnants of his saliva. The man pointed this out to the otter who promptly went down the hill to confront the locust.

The Ocean - *the emotional landscape of the unknown journey into the heart*

Water/Emotion

The boundless blue ocean lay under a clear blue sky, its calm surface concealing the force of movement and life beneath it. And as the sun lowered itself onto the distant horizon, dolphins celebrated jumping joyfully in arcs. The night descended quickly and an ominous feeling towards the expansive unknown became apparent. The waters were a powerful living force of mighty currents, with turbulence nearer to the shores. There was no light but the shimmer of the distant star's. The waves crashed loudly onto the shoreline, their presence a mere whisper from the ever shifting chanting mass; a negligible breath of reprieve.

All of this was present under a dark moonless sky. This living entity, so perfectly contained, with immeasurable depths and its life always continuing, both separate and connected.

A small golden fish swam alone along a current, feeling her way to her destination. And although it was dark she swam in what appeared to be a stream of light from on high, humming a tune, aware of the water supporting her along her path. Beneath her little side fins, she was able to sense the slightest shift in temperature and direction. She stayed within the song of her heart, knowing it would carry her home. She glanced from side to side, always aware of bigger fish than herself, and then returned once again to the song in her heart. Closing her eyes for a minute she allowed the feeling of homesickness to flow through her, the tears washing and clearing her eyes, and then taking a deep breath of immeasurable trust and feeling the support of the mighty ocean around her, she continued swimming forwards, her little body swaying from side to side.

Soon the sun would rise and everything would be clear.

The Whirlpool - *vortices of spiralling downward emotion have the capacity to connect us to the light*

Water/Emotion

A swirling whirlpool pulls downwards becoming larger and larger until it parts in the centre and there is air. The air is sucked downwards into the funnel, becoming a whirlwind being drawn towards the earth below. Then, the sand begins to spin and as the power of the maelstrom increases, the water carries the sand in circles and the air slowly burrows its way into the body.

This is the importance of the breath in the body being able to feed the cells of the body. The air burrows deeper and deeper into the stagnant, stuck energy of the floor of the earth which is then pushed into motion, circulating until a hollow thread of light is able to permeate. A good reminder to always return to the breath in times of overwhelming emotion, despite what one perhaps imagines to be the experience of a cyclone. Connect to the breath and permit the light to enter the body and clear out old stagnant energies, churning it and connecting the body to new light levels.

Stay in the breath, stay in the heart, stay connected.

Vortices have a function.

The Star - *connecting the light of the soul to the body, and bringing home here*

Fire/Spirit

A singular star, a spark of light in a dark night sky pulses gently, purposefully towards a destination far away. That destination is here. This light of my soul that I seek in a resonance I call home.

The twinkling stars glimmer in the open night sky, some are clear and near whilst others are distant and assembled. Each star emanates its own unique expression of light, simply being itself. They travel alone yet are connected to one another within unseen patterns of perfection which hold the larger design. All in motion and in relation to each other. Family. Sometimes the bulge of light in one group might press awkwardly upon its neighbours. A sphere within a cycle and circle, all floating in an empty timeless space.

And somewhere not too far away shines the gentle orange glow of one lone star, seemingly lost, yet steadily holding its light, almost nostalgically.

I draw nearer to the orange warmth and then gently break through an unseen barrier into what at first appears to be a ball of blue and white. Upon closer inspection, visible layers upon layers become apparent. Layers and levels of energetic structure all held together by patches of materialised density beneath.

And when travelling closer, yet through the layers, each with its own pressure and frequencies, a sense of a maze becomes evident. Passageways between time. This is existence. Appearing in a mist of building blocks, pathways and levels, within which to navigate.

Consciousness, densely pressed together and contained by the forces of nature.

There, with his hands pressed together in a prayer at the front of his heart, and a gentle knowing smile upon his lips, stood a little being. He had clear sparkly eyes and the infinite stretch of eternity within his gaze. He waited patiently, for within his heart was a prayer, a holy emanation of sounds and symbols sent forth into the unstoppable universe. It seemed that in that far away grand space of everything and nothing, this little voice, this squeak of existence, could hardly extend to anywhere as distant as the great beyond. Yet, within that knowing smile was the deepest trust, held as a star in his heart, the spark of light that was the very nature of his creation. He knew that out there shone the light of a star in the exact resonation of himself and that he was speaking from within this resonation. And that it too, was seeking him with precision.

He began to feel a sense of warmth and expansion from contact with the oncoming light, and then there was an inter weaving and click of connection. Facing his hands upwards he began to sing his gratitude for being heard, and then sitting down gently into the lotus position he took a deep breath and relaxed into his body. With a lengthy out breath, he consciously released the busyness he held.

Preparing himself to receive, he felt into the warmth of the light upon his body and began to relax and merge into it. He experienced being deeply loved, this ever moving flowing light of life, streaming onto and through him.

Within the light stream appeared floating dust particles, evidence of the earth surrounding him. He centred himself, connecting into the rhythm of his heartbeat, and felt an aliveness within his hands. From the centre of his right hand flowed a clockwise spiral of light and in his left hand arrived a counter-clockwise spiral of light. High above him flew a stork confirming his new beginnings and the birthing of this new aspect of his spirit. His heart felt light and joyful, his mind empty and still. He listened carefully for any sounds of nature around him, to affirm his connection to this living earth-plane. The voice of nature deeply resonated through him, giving him his wings. He deepened his breath focusing on one sound and becoming its consciousness, uniting with it in deep harmony. This expression of simply being and embodying sound and form, the voice of creation held in design. He felt the powerful force and essence of connection. He was a single part connected to the whole. So he expanded his listening to the chorus of singing voices, all collaborating in perfect harmony and balance. Settling into his light once again, he felt it flowing through him and into the earth beneath him, locking and uniting home far away. Here. Now.

The Stars and the Ocean - *alignment to the blueprint of creation with the Holy Spirit, and the Elemental Kingdom*

Fire/Spirit & Water/Emotion

A dimming sky over a dimming ocean as the remnants of the day's light dissolve into the night. Upon the surface of the ocean there is a ripple of awareness responding to the twinkling stars on high.

It is an aware stillness, an alert stillness to the ever descending light streams of each individual star, as well as to the collective patterns of constellations. Slowly the waters settle and the light begins to enter. It is welcomed and ignites fluorescent, joyful patches within the dark waters. Within these giddy patches of light, life expresses itself in song and movement.

Inside a deep circle of light near the surface of the darkened body of water, an effervescent joyfulness exists, a reflection of the starlight above. And although this appears as a muted glow upon the surface of the ocean, with a closer eye the depth of the light is evident, clear and crystalline.

Within this light in the ocean is a little worm like creature with a gentle, peaceful voice and a twinkle in his eye. He says he knows many things that he has brought with him from his travels in far away places. He whispers them quietly as a soul story that echoes within the darkness and is carried upon the winds. His little hands are placed together at his heart, waiting graciously for acknowledgment.

He is unlike the caterpillar who has many legs to lean upon carrying his many lives; who wears a top hat, tails and a walking stick, emanating the charm of a well accomplished showman. For the caterpillar, the response of an audience is always a great delight and pleasing affirmation to his existence. He is forever seeking the spotlight and applause.

When this little worm-like creature receives acknowledgement, he simply smiles a deep knowing smile, the gentle smile of his heart. For within the silence of this boundless ocean where the stars have made a spotlight on this little patch of water, where a gentle slapping can be heard above and the rhythmic sway of back and forth, side to side, he is now home.

He waits patiently with his hands facing upwards, receiving the sparkles of light falling through the water. His hands capture the light igniting his little heart and causing ripples of delight to flow through and out of his body. And with his focus on receiving this light he is able to begin a pulse from his heart that encourages his body to gently begin to glow, lighting the space around him. His hands tingle and his entire body proceeds to come to life, the electrical current finding a pathway into existence. He claps his hands high in front of him giving praise to the Holy Spirit of the Light for its blessings, and then begins a joyful dance. The ever descending flow of light washes over and around him, witness to his success and joy.

Finally, feeling his joy subside to a steady blissful pulse he comes into stillness with his hands together at his heart and his eyes closed. He listens attentively to the voice in his heart and then says, 'It is done.' Sitting once again in the Lotus position with his hands gently resting upon his knees facing upward, he closes his eyes and breathes into that holy space within his heart, his Temple. And from his Temple emanates a steady stream of light creating a sphere around him.

Home has finally arrived. Here.

The Forest

I looked at the forest covering the hills in the dusky light, as the day completed and the stars appeared above in the night sky. The light seemed to be whizzing its way through the empty space in a buzz of determination, its destination the forest. I noticed a small bullet type object battering itself against an invisible crystalline barrier in the space, its frustration and perseverance admirable, but to no avail. The light frequencies continued to effortlessly fall through space sweeping past the object into the protected interior.

The forest was a living, breathing entity of its own, containing the designs of creation materialised into form. Each green leaf was a little spirit celebrating its capacity to be in this plane of existence whilst happily watching the evolution of life surrounding it. Honoured to be a part of it all.

I peered into the eye of the little spirit on top of a leaf and it blinked, looking back at me. We were both curious about each other. It unexpectedly blew some air in my face surprising me, and I quickly pulled back. Perhaps I had gotten too close. I bent down to take a closer look into its eye again. Suddenly there were two eyes and a chubby round little figure standing on the leaf in front of me with arms bent and hands on its hips. It crooked its finger on its left hand beckoning me closer, as if to whisper in my ear. I leaned in and heard the words, 'You are lovely'. Receiving them in my heart, I placed my hands together in front of my heart in appreciation. Then opening my eyes and leaning away a little I blew gold dust off the tops of my hands, to shroud the little being in its glow. He clapped his hands merrily doing a little dance in a circle and singing a song of celebration. The birds in the trees caught the song in the wind, responding in a joyful chorus of sound.

Laying down gently upon the cool earth in the shade of the forest I felt into my heartbeat and then connected to the gentle pulse of the earth beneath me. We were one. My breath seemed to be the breath of the forest and all the living beings were witness to this moment as a part of the nature of my existence. I sunk deeper into the cool surface at my back and focused upon my breath, becoming aware that above the forest were clear blue skies and an empty space for the light to flow. I am this breath of light, I am this forest, the earth is beneath me and I am supported by her. I am here.

The Eagle and the Forest - *higher perspective of the light materialised into form as seen in the Garden of Eden, following the key story to the creational process, the Tree of Life*

Earth/Physical & Air/Mental

The eagle soared high in a clear blue sky, observing with its golden all-seeing eye of truth and understanding. It slowly lowered the course of its flight onto a new pattern of design unseen to the naked eye within the air. He circled in wide infinity arcs, parallel to the earth-plane.

His gaze swept the broad picture below observing with detailed focus the unfolding story of its nature, as one would read a book. He noted everything from the community of ants building their homes, each individual called into being with its unique gifts to the whole, to the rhino defending its territory with a defensive-aggressive embodiment.

And within the dark centre of the eagle's eye reflected the expansive space of the universe above him, where the patterns of the stars held the stories of this materialised creation below. These were the light designs that contained the foundation for his higher perspective, the patterns from which his all-seeing eye could intuit the book below.

The jungle of green trees was a rich texture of brush and life with patterns of growth all reaching upwards. The eagle's heart responded to the outreach, to the mighty green love for the light. This light that descended into the nature of being. It was a uniting of magical spirit and form under what appeared to be an empty blue sky.

The golden-yellow eyes of the eagle glowed appreciatively for this living transforming existence. Which could be seen as a mirror reflected on the dark pupil of his eye. The designs of the light of the stars glimmered as the green of life on earth. Each design was a manifestation of the spirit of the divine nature of the Creator's heart. The fleshy patterns drank the light with an insatiable thirst, materialising his holy spirit into form.

The eagle floated down and landed on a branch feeling the hum of life breathing through the tree and flowing up and out through him. He could feel this love of being, this song of the heart. And all of these songs of the forest together in a harmonic chorus of response to the stars above.

He closed his eyes focusing on his heartbeat whilst his wings gently tremored in the vibration of sound flowing through him, and his soul elevated in the echo. Breathing in the light, he gently pulled himself back into his body feeling its rhythmic surges. It felt good to be here, to feel this pulse of life giving him strength and to remember himself in physical form. He could remember from this perspective his ability to soar between the layers above, simply feeling and trusting the way. The creative patterns within the unseen flow of the skies and beneath his wings, always guiding him home.

With his eyes closed and his ears focused on the steady beat within the centre of his heart, he felt as one with the earth, her pulse, his. As the earth soaked up the light, always reaching higher and higher, - her creation became an expression of the eternal dance into being.

Stretching out his wings he felt the cool breath beneath them, and became aware of the subtle frequencies and flow that were inviting him upward. It was time to detach and separate himself from his connection to the tree. With his attachment to the tree his heart felt so peaceful and connected to all of existence, he was magnetised to the whole. It was an experience of co-existence, to rest and feel supported.

With a deep inhalation he pressed his wings down onto the beat of the mother earth's heart, and powerfully lifted himself from the earth-plane to soar free, to reach a higher perspective. Where he could see the picture from above, separated and soaring along the unseen designs of perfection, feeling them shift and change beneath his wings. All the while observing the forest below.

5

CHaracTers anD ArcHeTyPes

Characters, as Characteristics of Self

The Great Mother - *nourishing and nurturing oneself*

Mother Mary holds the Christed child in her arms gazing deeply into his eyes, her heart filled with love, her bare feet upon the earth. She is swathed in robes of blue material, her child in her arms protected with a coronet of white. The baby is firmly supported in her arms whilst the eyes of the father watch carefully as they bond, mother and child's hearts uniting.

Very soon the baby becomes a toddler, wild and free, running upon the earth towards the forest and all of its life. In the wild green garden of the forest, he speaks with the animals and creatures listening to their stories, and becoming their friend. They tell him what he can eat when he is hungry and where to go when he is lost, and how to find the clear waters of the river when he is thirsty. At the waters he is also able to speak with the fish.

Slowly he grows into a strong, handsome young man with feathers in his hair, adorning tribal cloth, his feet bare upon the fertile soils. He knows that from these soils he is fed and clothed, and that the clear blue skies above give him fresh air and the warmth of the sun. He breathes it all in, with immense gratitude in his heart for his home here, with this Great Being.

The Great Father - *trusting oneself to provide and protect*

The light of creation rises behind the indigo mountains; those original patterns in the most dense materialised form. Its warmth and blessings birth green sprouts of life everywhere.

The Father of light and love speaks words of love and en-**courage**ment, his sacred sounds holy emanations of creations evolution. His pure heart of truth and reason enables vision, and enlightenment to a heart's dream across the landscapes of creation.This is the light of our soul beaming down upon the earth-plane, warm and alive, and forever drawing life upwards.

Growth.

Father Sun, relentlessly shines his light and warmth, his love onto mother earth. She responds with her magnificent nature. For within this light are the patterns of creation upon which our evolution depends. This golden light is the light that we are. It is the light that materialises into the Gold connection to this Golden Age of Light.

The Pure, Innocent and Magical Little Girl - *that part of ourselves that we trust*

The pure, innocent and magical little girl who is the apple of her fathers eye, never falling far from the tree. The fruit seeds itself again and again with the tree always bearing sweet fruit under the warmth and light of the sun. A tree that blossoms in the springtime with the promise of new life. She is the true alchemist, whom we completely trust. She is the divine feminine, innocently receiving her pure light from the Creator. She is usually under the age of seven.

The feminine is the energy of creation and the masculine is creation in action. Being and doing. In order to create in alignment with the Divine we need to receive our light-stream, to embody it, and create within the laws of nature. We need to trust ourselves to be able to do this.

The Magical Boy - *the part of ourselves we trust to give ourselves what we need and get things done*

He stands upon Jacob's ladder leaning against the moon in the dark of night. He peers out into the universe, seeking the designs of his heart that he wishes to return to the earthplane. This is the divine nature of his heart. He does what needs to be done and gives us what we need.

He leans Jacob's ladder against the moon and then climbs up it, peering out into the universe to the patterns beyond, that need to be returned here. The moonlight shines into the dark unknown, the unseen parts of ourselves that need to be illuminated. Raising the unconscious into consciousness.

Grandfather - *the heart of deep knowing*

The lizard lay in the sun on the desert landscape listening within the stillness to the subtle shifting air streams. For within the unseen patterns above, beneath the clear blue sky, were magnificent designs of crystal creation descending onto the earth.

Grandfather breathed in deeply as he sat on the porch outside his front door. The porch overlooked the forest beneath him and his pond on the hilltop to the East. He loved this place with the chattering forest and magical light above, where he was King of the pond.

The frog sat on the lotus leaf in the still waters of the pond, his crown propped firmly upon his head. He closed his normally alert eyes, breathing deeply into his chest and feeling into the foundation of the pond. Here, he could connect to the heart-beat of the Great Mother and feel her kind stories. She had a heart of forgiveness, wisdom and truth and she was the great love of his life. She was the reason he existed. Her stories were his stories, her landscapes were his landscapes, and her heart was merely a reflection of his own. He smiled lovingly, holding the connection with intention, remembering his purpose. Staying in his heart.

Grandmother - *the heart of understanding*

Within the see-saw of her heart and the twinkle in her ancient blue eyes, Grandmother rocked in her chair in the left corner of the empty white room. Her hands were relaxed on top of the slender wooden arms of the chair, wrinkled with thick blue veins. She had the eyes of one who has the patience of an eternal heart, biding her time in the forwards and backwards, up and down motion of life.

Closing her eyes she placed her hands over her heart feeling into the heavy weight that underlay the oscillation, and then getting up she exited the house from the front door.

Outside was a clear blue sky that was clouding over quickly, the light changing over the undulating hills below. The hills were covered in an old forest of dark green trees and the house faced West into the setting sun. The round yellow sun was paused over the hills, casting long dark shadows of gloom and surrender.

The old woman gazed acceptingly at the picture before her, understanding how quickly a landscape can shift and change. This was the landscape of this now-moment of being. Here. Inevitable.

She inhaled deeply, placing her left hand over her heart once again, feeling the last warmth of the weak rays of the sun on her face. A cool breeze fanned her skin and she became aware of her breathing. With each breath she dropped into the slow steady beat of her heart.

She noticed that she was wearing grey pumps with a heel to raise her vision slightly. And as she breathed carefully into this exact moment of awareness, her surroundings stood still in time and she imagined the moonless night sky with its infinite display of stars shining down upon this place.

The first thing she noticed was that the house was gone and only nature encircled her. She saw vertical threads of streaming light connecting every form on the earth-plane to each individual star. It appeared as if every structure came from an individual light source. The dark shapes of expression were simply patterned shadows emerging from a flat landscape. The dark structures were receiving the light streams and absorbing them. They appeared to be standing still in an eternal, now-moment where horizontal grids of connection held the entire manifestation in place. The horizontal grids appeared more faintly than the forms, and were lighter in emanation. The grids accommodated each shape within its specific level and frequency of vibration. They were silver and gold and shimmered exquisitely with an inaudible sound. When she looked to see what was holding the grids in place, she noticed how they continued across the land towards the ocean. Here they settled under the reflection of a full moon, and then disappeared into the infinite horizon.

A dolphin arced joyfully across the silvery stream of moonlight and then re-entered its silky liquid interior. The dolphin's eyes were earthy brown intelligence and the arc of her movement into the air was the same curve that she undulated along within the waters.She voiced her recognition and greeting of seeing and being seen. The shape of her body lent itself to the curve of the circles of time. She would effortlessly swim in ascending spirals of connection until she reached the surface of the water, where she was able to inhale the lightness and release herself into the majestic blue heavens.

The pressure of the water on her body, while a form of support, also created influence upon her. She loved to free herself from it when ascending into the air above.

She accepted that this was her home, these curved lines of connection and undulating horizontal threads of light which she swam upon, singing her holy songs of truth.

Her heavy heart felt the pressure of the waters, the weight of the ocean and her knowing of travel along the lines ahead. Always moving forward into what felt like the infinite known unknown.

Grandmother returned to her rocking chair in the corner of the empty white room. On her left was a vibrant fire burning in the fireplace, bringing flickering light and warmth into the room. She rested her palms together in her lap and closed her eyes feeling the backwards and forwards swaying, the motion of being here. She smiled gently to herself in acceptance of this place in her heart, simply breathing into it and allowing the motion to follow through. Simply breathing.

The Magician - *trickster, alchemist and entertainer*

Dressed in black with a sparkle in his eye and a heart of conviction. He has an ace up his sleeve, this is his mastery. He entertains the little girl with his tricks, his heart animated by his skill.

The magician is an alchemist capable of trickery. A master in the art of concealing and deception, but wonderfully entertaining.

A good teacher and not to be entirely trusted.

The Witch - *studies empowerment*

With her hooked nose, bent shoulders and cackling laugh, she peers at life with a heart of malice. Accompanied by her pointed hat, black cloak and broom, she flies across the night sky.

This alchemist is capable of brewing many concoctions, both light and dark.

The Medicine Woman - *healing self*

Bent over her bowl at the fire in the centre of the medicine wheel, she speaks with the nature spirits willing them to obey her commands. She is always learning. Her spirit is aligned with the stars. She has the ability to miraculously heal using her wisdom of the Nature Spirits.

Much karma has been created through miscreation of this knowledge. We break our trust within ourselves through the use of dark magic, abusing the nature spirits and abusing our magical connection to the elemental kingdom of our beloved Mother. And so we lose our ability to 'see' the magical kingdom of the Garden of Eden.

The Genie - *the genius in our heart*

The golden heart of wisdom within the dark night of the universe, the cave of consciousness wherein the genie appears when summoned.

Within each of us is the Genius, the Genie. He lives in the cave deep within our hearts and the truth of our Being. In order to access him, we need to 'rub the lamp' or activate the light within our soul, and trust our own inner wisdom.

The King/Queen - *self empowered, sovereign beings connected to the Kingdoms of Heaven*

The Golden Crown embellished with jewels of wisdom, reigning over the kingdom of its creation, with a golden heart of Love.

The King/Queen archetypes are about self empowerment. The golden bejewelled crown is also the crown chakra and reveals the many levels and layers of empowerment.

They rule over the castle of our consciousness, home in our hearts connected to the kingdoms of heaven.

The Three Fold Flame - *our power to move forward*

The golden fleur-de-lis is embossed upon royal fabric. White satin material shining beneath the golden emblem glinting in the light. The blue, pink and gold rays of the sunrise announce the beginning of a new day showered in golden rays of sunlight, as well as the completion at the end of a day. The golden age of wisdom arrives with a pink heart of loving compassion, and the blue skies of freedom above. It is our Will. The golden chariot is driven by a strong man in control of six horses, and who uses his will power to guide his vehicle. His vehicle is a six pointed star in the night sky.

Sunset and Sunrise - the nature of the kundalini

Completion and New Beginnings, sunsets and sunrises, which are the colours of the Three Fold Flame of transformation. This flame is also known as the Fleur-de-lis which we see on Royal Fabric. This translates to the Lotus or Lily Flower - our ability to connect to our crystalline DNA, 'Om Mane Padme Hum' - I am the jewel in the Lotus Flower.

The colours of these rays of light or flames are the process that we follow in order to transform our suffering into wisdom. We use our **willpower**, the blue ray to breathe into **compassion**, the pink ray as this ray has a higher frequency than the suffering. Within our compassion we find acceptance of the experience we are going through, understanding of what we have learned from it and forgiveness for creating such suffering. What we have learned from this experience is the gold, our **wisdom**.

The nature of the serpent, our kundalini, to move forward is to oscillate West and East, sunset and sunrise or completion and new beginnings. This is when we are self empowered on our journeys, the King and Queen archetypes. We are self empowered sovereign beings of the light propelling our souls evolution forward. It all begins with willpower, the blue ray which is also the colour of heaven. Our freedom on earth.

The Warrior - one who is willing to go to war

Protected within his metal garments, he raises his right arm to the heavens calling forth the armies of light with his powerful voice.

He appears as a robust man with a horned helmet and metal attire.

He protects us, allowing us to feel safe for our soul's evolution.

An armoured knight appears upon his black horse, ready for battle.

Behind him a tornado spins across the empty landscape moving with speed towards the East. The knight is aware of it but waits on his horse for a sign from above.

Blue skies surround him and white butterflies flutter about his horse's legs. He is hot and sweating beneath the metal, becoming increasingly uncomfortable in his attire.

What is he really waiting for, he wonders. An instruction? He climbs off the horse and frees himself from his protective covering feeling the gentle swish of the air upon his skin, the hairs on his arms responding.

He breaths into the feeling of freedom from the weight of his garments, the weight of expectation for the role of the warrior.

Laying himself down upon the white sandy earth under the blue skies, he closes his eyes and smells the delicate scent of the flowers making a groundcover around him. It is a faint scent joined by the buzz of bees and other insects. He feels the warmth of the sun on his skin and brings his awareness to the distant tornado. Better to lay low here than be in the path of that tornado, he thinks. Its nature is to destroy all that is in its path, until it has exhausted itself.

He brings himself into presence once more, feeling the peaceful existence of nature surrounding him, and his liberation from his garments. His heart is light, his breath even and the earth supports his back. He smiles.

6

STORIES

The Lost Politician *- power struggles*

A reptilian lizard with shifting eyes. Demonic, red glowing eyes which when clear, reveal his presence swaying between the worlds. He holds both clarity and confusion, and the lostness in-between. He is always seeking something to hold onto. Living between the dark and the light, lost in between.

Perhaps seeking power is the solution to believe in. It can give him a position, somewhere within a structure, a ladder to climb. The opportunity to dominate.

Yet constantly there is someone more powerful and someone less powerful, and he is always in-between. Going somewhere, leaving somewhere, striving to be somewhere else. Imagining his gifts are being useful, yet knowing ultimately he is being destructive as he clears the path before him by destroying that which is in his way. A pathway of destruction perceived to be moving upwards. Clawing within the ranks of corruption. Paid for with destructive, disruptive chemicals that interfere with consciousness. Disempowering to empower.

And in his heart, a deep feeling of betrayal of the truth and purity of his Being. With every step he takes into the dark destruction towards a material ladder of success, his spirit sinks into the depths beneath, further from the lightness of his soul. And the demons strengthen their grip, with their promised cage of protection - now a cage of separation. His heart is alone, yearning to be acknowledged, and he is trapped in a jail of discontent and frustration, with nothing but emptiness surrounding him.

Sitting with his head in his hands, he traces his steps to this place, accounting for every decision he fell victim to. His imagined destination of glory on a stage of appreciation, protected by those that love him. But where was any love in this game? Love for power and recognition. A stage to be seen - with claws waiting in the wings.

A puppet to the mastery of self delusion, to a heart that seeks to be seen. A heart that seeks itself in its audience, imagining respect; knowing truth.

The doctor, healing others of their attachments to their own darkness, worthy in their eyes, but never making time to look within. It's too painful.

Rather to manipulate the world around him than to see the sad lostness within.

Until sitting in the cage of his own creation, trapped and alone, he opens the door to the audience of expectation, waiting for applause but in the mirror of faces only seeing denial, and feeling the prickle of claws at his back.

Where were the faces of hope and trust? His promise of a solution.

And remembering his path, each step a choice, his trust and hope were broken, his heart an empty promise.

This stage - a spotlight of truth.

If I cannot save myself, how can I save you?

Go home and seek the hero within, I am not that person you seek.

Lady Liberty - *the capacity to free oneself*

An angel appears before me in the higher realms. It is Lady Liberty wearing white feathered wings. She is clothed in a long blue dress with a gold sash at her waist, a golden wreath of leaves around her head, and in her upright extended hand, she holds the flame of liberation.

She looks into my eyes quizzically as if to make sure I understand why she is here, confirming that I am ready to consciously release and liberate myself. I close my eyes, placing my right hand over my left upon my heart. I tune into my heart's bearing. It feels as if I have been carrying a deep heartsore for all of eternity. I cannot remember a time when it was not there, certainly not in this lifetime. I feel the tears welling up from my crying heart, the overwhelming sadness of my being. It is as if I have been addicted to this feeling and have forgotten that I have the choice to let it go. It is not all that I am, it is merely one portion of a greater whole.

I open my eyes and look into the depth of hers, seeing the perfection of a night sky. First, I see a hawk. Then I see a crocodile pulling an enormous serpent from a tall tree and destroying it. My reptilian brain, the fearful protection of my heart and the unmoving life force attached to my tree of life. The vertical weight of this beast has been blocking me, disconnecting my ability to move forward.

I inhale and let go, feeling a sense of release and relief from the heartsore, the heavy weight of that serpent stuck in my central design. I notice how light I feel, unblocked with a toroidal outward flow. My energy feels balanced on my shoulders, with my heart centred in between.

Lady Liberty stands before me to the North. She tips her torch, dropping a large flame of fire into my central axis. I feel it burn its way through, dissolving irregularities as I draw a deep breath inwards, welcoming it through my being. She then begins to walk in a counter clockwise direction and I hear her voice of liberation, freeing me from this addiction of mine. I open my heart and receive her blessings as she bows outwards to each direction. She is requesting the design be held in place throughout space and time.

I place my hands together at my heart in appreciation and acknowledgment of her grace, with tears behind my eyes for her compassion. This divine moment has arrived because I am ready to experience a new way of being. I am liberated from the old stories that were trapping me. I feel my white feathered wings attached to my back, my golden halo containing my central flow of light and the steady rhythm of my heart connecting me into this plane of existence.

I am in a small rowboat on a large expanse of water, wherein I see golden symbols written reflecting the heavens. The gently undulating waves move the golden light of the symbols in perfect flow. I am free on this ocean of water under the heavens, and although the skies are cloudy, I can manage. I feel a cool, moist breeze on my face.

This heart of mine, free by redemption and the blessings of Lady Liberty. She, who walks with me and knows my heart as her own. Knows all that I have learned and completed.

I hold the wisdom of my journey with so much love. I no longer choose that suffering heart for it has disconnected me from my flow and full expression of being here. I am here, connected into this plane of existence uniting into the frequencies of nature. The nature spirits hold me, unveiling themselves, so joyful and compassionate.

A gentle pink sunrise appears to the East, as the stars begin to fade. It is the dawning of a new day with clear blue skies above.

A yellow daisy appears on the green hillside, awakening joyfully to the light upon the green undulating waves of my heart.

The Self Saboteur - *self destructive behaviour*

The self sabotaging feminine who hangs herself, preventing breath and connection. She hangs from the hangman's gallows, her fingers clawing at the noose around her neck as she struggles to breathe. Her little girl is standing on the platform to the left side of her dangling, jerking body.

The little girl's arms are crossed over her chest as she waits for the struggle to cease, for this internal war within her mother to resolve. The mother fails to give her little girl the attention she needs. Distraught, she turns inward, although still aware of the little girl standing at her side. She focuses with all of her might at the restriction she feels around her throat, this silencing of her voice. Why has she arrived in this place, and how did she get herself here?

She descends into her heart where there is confusion and many demanding voices asking her questions and giving her instructions. With so much noise around her she knows that the answer is to take time and seek the inward path to her temple. A temple that is white, with purple and gold finishes, and provides transmutation through the highest connecting frequencies of golden light.

She sits down into the lotus position in the centre of the structure. Then, breathing deeply into her heart she seeks that still place where she can receive answers, consciously ignoring the raucous discord around her.

Her vision opens and she sees a worm under the ground, evidence of something in her physical body creating disruption. Its eyes are closed as it lies curled into a spiral of connection, engorged and white. The liquid in the worm's body is absorbing the frequencies around it and soaking up the patterns of her creation. It is taking all of her hard work for its own potential growth. It is a self-serving vampire. Using her will power, she forces it out, dissolving it into the light, and then repeats the process three more times. With the intention of clearing her energy she continues, until she feels a sense of deep peacefulness wash over and through her, covering her in a blanket of tranquillity.

She says a prayer of gratitude to the high heavens for their assistance in making her aware of her state of discomfort. For helping her find the willpower to look more deeply into herself and find the issue, then willingly release it.

The mother stands next to the little girl on the ground. She looks at the little girl without defending herself, for she has had a difficult journey. Then, taking the little girl's left hand into her own, they walk up the hill together, to a house filled with glass windows and light, in the centre of a wild green garden.

The Medicine Woman, the Ship's Captain and the Goat - *the characters that work together to bring healing*

Within the centre of our hearts is a circular empty space from which 12 threads of light emanate outwards. An echo of the medicine wheel, the steering wheel of a ship and the dharma wheel.

Within this central space exists the medicine woman and the captain of the ship. Their relationship is an important one, for the medicine woman instructs the captain of the boat in the dark of night to seek that which she requires in order to heal. The captain has the capacity to read the starry night sky and navigate the ship to the required destination.

As it is the nature of a goat to effortlessly summit a steep rocky mountain eating nutritious medicinal herbs along its way, such is the nature of the medicine woman. She points her finger in the direction of the constellations towards a specific design, a pattern of light that needs to be returned to the body to hea l.With pinpoint precision, the captain steers the boat through the spaces in between, to arrive at the given destination.

Each plant, a medicinal herb on the mountain, contains the divine patterning of the perfection of creation materialised and rooted into the earthplane. The goat simply devours the patterns connecting him to his journey as he climbs each mountain, higher and higher.

The medicine woman points to the horizon at the setting sun, the very same spot as the setting full moon. In the ambient pink dusky light, she senses into her heart with its steady beat; her love and compassion seeking a cure for an affliction. With the medicine wheel in her heart, the rays of light illuminating the universe within, she gives the captain the coordinates of the exact time/space location. With the captain's mastery over the waters, between the dimensions and timelines, grids upon grids of existence; he navigates his way to these stars.

The stars beam their brilliant light, singing their divine song into the vessel.

And a blue sparrow lands upon the vessel, but for a brief moment.

The King and the Queen Blueprints of Creation

In a deck of cards, the King and the Queen are at the top, as the self empowered masculine and feminine. They give birth to the son/sun/soul, the light of creation. Thereafter follows the divine patterning of numbers, beneath them. The science and mathematics of this Universe is in perfection with the different combinations of numbers or possible experiences, being infinite. With an empowered and balanced masculine and feminine ruling over the deck, the potential patterns and formations become aligned with the patterning of the universe itself. One's experience of materialised reality is united with the heavens, following the Law of 'As above so Below.'

The King - *the self empowered masculine*

Once upon a time in a far away land, where the trees were golden and the skies were blue, a temple floated in the air appearing as a palace, and unicorns roamed the infinite blue yonder.

The King of the castle, who wore a black and white soft warm robe with a purple sash around his neck, opened the castle door. He was a gallant and noble man with warm twinkly blue eyes. He supervised the growth of the orchards of golden trees, his warm and loving heart caring for them as his children. Upon opening the castle door he greeted a unicorn at the entrance, then placing his hands together at his heart he bowed his head in appreciation of her arrival. He rubbed her neck, fondly knowing that she had come to show him a vision. Placing her horn gently between his eyes, she sent forth spirals of flowing rainbow light, opening the timelines and dimensions.

Through the cycles and circles of existence, the King saw the back of a man dressed in black walking alone down a dusty road. The King moved himself in consciousness that he might watch the man from the front. He noticed that the small figure was rubbing his hands together and speaking to himself. He was telling himself that it was a 'good plan, a great plan,' while tapping the right side of his head with his right hand, and then pointing his index finger in front of him as if he was explaining it to somebody. The little man crossed his arms across his solar plexus in a protective and self satisfied manner, then he raised his hands to the heavens and cried, 'Great Spirit, I hope you are hearing my request, that I might walk along this road between fields of red Poppies, smelling the sweetness of life and seeing your magnificence gently swaying in the breeze against the eternal blue skies. He felt the light of Great Spirits love gently warming his back.

Before him appeared the unicorn, brilliant white with rainbows of etheric light emanating from her horn.

'What are you asking for?' she questioned him.

'Fields of red flowers blooming in the warmth of the golden sun, the light glowing orange through their translucent petals' he replied.

'Why are you dressed in black?' she asked.

'I want to use the flowers for a specific purpose,' the little man said.

The unicorn replied, 'need I remind you that the lower chakras are all the colours of the fiery flames of transformation and that Mother Nature and the Heavens above begin at the Green chakra of the Heart.'

'But all of nature is in perfection' said the little man, 'and the red poppies have magical gifts.'

Yes, the flowers ground the lower chakras allowing the spirit to soar. For the little man understood the principle of 'as low as you go is as high as you go.' He continued to walk with a lightness to his step for in his mind's eye the vision had already materialised, he understood that **vision created reality**. Beating his heart with his right hand, his body smiled and his spirit raised.

Fields of Poppies where there is nothing but an empty landscape, seemed a plan of the Gods.

'Why do you need fields?' asked the unicorn.

'To reach many people I will need many poppy's, the magic of the flowers is as infinite as humans.' The unicorn began to walk alongside the little man dressed in black.

'Are the sight and smell of the flowers not enough?' she asked. 'Why do you want to use the magic of her spirit to create more than what is here? Is here not enough?' There was a falter in his step.

'I give you a warning' said the unicorn, 'there is a law in this universe, that what you do to others can be done to you. If you should use the nature of the spirit of the poppy to shift your experience of the nature of your reality, you open yourself up to the same. You give permission to Beings that believe that you are useful, to do the same to you. It is unwise to believe that you are the top of the hierarchy. Consciousness is ever expansive and is stepped all the way down to the earth plane. The unseen world, the world at a higher frequency of light, watches and learns too. The Laws stay the same. What you do to others can be done unto you.'

She turned to the little man, 'now look into your heart and ask yourself, would you like someone to use the magical nature of your spirit to enhance the personal reality of their existence? For with your plan, your permission is given. It is simply a plan of disempowerment, nothing else. Be aware.'

The King bowed deeply to the Unicorn, his hands together at his heart, with gratitude and appreciation for her gift. She turned and swiftly flew beyond. Her vision was through all lines of time, she held the infinite awareness of all that is.

He entered the castle once again, closing the front door behind him, and reluctantly removed his purple sash. The time had arrived for the return of his presence to the earth-plane, once more. For the power of the King to walk upon the lands respect-fully in wonder, amongst the nature spirits.

For his understanding and appreciation of their power, was his understanding and appreciation of his own.

The Queen - *the self empowered feminine, queen of your heart*

The Queen wears her magnificent golden crown of glory; golden scallops tipped with pearls of wisdom. The central gem on the front of her crown is an oval emerald of the heart, with triangular facets of balance.

Within each of our hearts is this same courage that comes with balance and empowerment, that we seek during times of perceived chaos. To stand firm, knowing the power we have to create our own hearts dream. To trust ourselves as creator beings of the light, with the dignity, understanding and deeply understanding heart, of the Queen.

Her confident hand glides over the lands of her kingdom, radiating the same golden light as her heart. She whispers warm words of comfort, soothing the fears of the uncertain heart.

The surface of the heart has forgotten this wisdom so deeply buried within the body, the original divine perfection of creation to which we once again return. The divine self-empowered Earth.

Within the DNA and cells are unforgotten codes of creation, patterns of perfection in light waves of the divine. Soul song signatures co-creating in a chorus of harmonic bliss. Independent sounds uniting with each other to become a chorus of earthly Angels, connected to the heart of creation, the creator.

As individuals each of us learns to walk with a heart of compassion, a heart knowing deeply of earthly suffering, a heart of forgiveness. We trust that upon this illuminating pathway into what sometimes appears as a cloudy heaven, our heart beats are one with the heart of creation, the heart of the creator.

Within the eternal soul we are connected all the way from source, stepping our way down onto the earth-plane through many planes of existence. Mirrors of learning that light this pathway of conscious awakening, inviting each and every one of us to find our way home. Home in our heart. We are invited to discover that place where the skies are filled with rainbows as soul agreements come to fruition and the heavens become clear. A place in our hearts where we can hear the summons from the chorus of creation. And as each of us listens carefully, opening the temple within our hearts to these compelling sounds, we are able to respond to this call home, we are able to respond with the song in our heart.

As compassion, understanding and forgiveness arrive, the Queen's higher earthly vision awakens, and she is reminded of the celebrations of her heart, of happier times. The King stands to her right side holding her hand, their fingers entwined, as they firmly face East towards the dawning of a new day. Where the ever strengthening light draws their souls forward, dissolving the shadows of the past and warming their bodies with a promise of solace.

Within each of our hearts is the Queen of hearts, the one who knows of the heartsore, the bleeding heart, the broken heart. She holds within her compassion for the suffering of others because she knows her own suffering so well. Placing her right hand upon her heart, she bows her head to it, in acknowledgment and appreciation for all that she has endured upon this earth-plane and the strength it has given her.

Raising her arms to the heavens she exhales a breath of gratitude, for within her kingdom, the golden fields of wheat are growing, ready to be shared with the children of many households. And from the golden light of the sun these fields received their nourishment and are now a gift to the bodies of all God's children, bringing heaven to earth.

The Beloved - *our natural design as the Tree of Life*

The Green Leaves on the trees shine brightly in the sunlight, they are receiving as much light as they can, as much love as they can, this light and love of creation. The light bounces off the leaves into its surroundings in joyful celebration. Limitless light filling the air like an overripe fruit bursting with juiciness and flavour, flavour that the mouth is yearning for a taste of. It is golden, platinum and diamond and exudes the perfume of the Ancients, teasing the senses to awaken.

But the weight of the dark blanket of remembering, of holding on to the past, visiting and revisiting the old, old stories again and again. Bringing them back into the heart, feeling to snuggle under this blanket of darkness, imagining it to be a blanket of comfort for the soul. This empty dark space simply being the familiar, the family of the past.

I take a deep breath into the heart, into my heartsore. That empty dark space where there is nothing but the grip of darkness, and I breathe into acceptance of what is there. This is in me and I have imagined it is my comfort.

And now, breathing in through the nose I imagine I am inhaling the light that exists around a little spark of light within my heart, simply a spark nothing more. For this little spark of light brought me into creation, and it is connected to a star in the heavens. It is connected to the light of the creation of my soul that feels so far away. Nevertheless, I am connected through all time and space. It is the eternal, the earth and the spirit that I am. Connected to all the other stars in the universe also shining their light onto the earthplane, sharing their boundless love.

The trees receive this light of my spirit upon the earth, until this light of God within me remembers to reconnect with the source of my creation.

There is an effervescent thread of light flowing upwards from my heart with white feathered wings and arms outstretched embracing the world. This is the nature of my spirit yearning to embrace all of life, all of my love for creation. This thread of light streams upwards from my heart seeking home far away.

Being aware of this spark of light in my heart, I request the light of my star, to return and reconnect with my heart; that heaven can return to earth.

'Come home, come home, come home, reunite my spirit with the earth-plane, for I am grounded, here, now and need to feel the lightness of my spirit, the wings of freedom once again.'

The wide embrace of my love emanates from my outstretched arms in gratitude to the trees for patiently waiting for me to remember and seek re-connection. That my thread of light can reunite with the frequency of home, holding the same beat as my heart and the same song of my soul.

With spirals of light flowing upwards, both clockwise and counter-clockwise, I seek the sound of my creation so far away, the song of my soul so endless and pure. And within the eternal dark blanket of space there is a connection in frequency, like two lovers joining hands. It is the heart of creation responding to my call. A winged white horse of deliverance travels through space towards the light of this soul upon the earth, bringing with him a thread of light from the star. It is the outstretched arms of the creator embracing his child within the circle of his love. My heart is home, in the light of God once again.

The leaves on the tree are the deep green of mother nature, of my heart chakra. They know this light feeds them. The leaves nourish the branches, the body and the roots of the tree. Light is the food of their very existence and the leaf knows how to convert light into food. The heart of the body knows this too and it is time to reconnect to my soul light, to reunite with the starlight in the dark space of existence that seems so far away.

I breathe quietly into the knowing of that little spark of creation that I am and remember where I come from calling myself back. Home is here now, within what sometimes feels like lost space and time but is really just a moment, an opportunity to find that voice in my heart.

The cry of my heart carried forth into the dark space of the universe is simply a question seeking an answer, and now it is time to receive.

Breathing in, I open my heart to receive the light, knowing that my call has been heard and it is my free will to open my heart and receive the answer.

Within each heart is a song of joy for the dawning of a new day, for the arrival of the light after a dark night. The light arrives without permission.

The sun will rise and shine his love, what I do with this - is my own choice.

On this planet of Free Will it takes willpower to will the heart into receiving the love that it has been created with. That it has forgotten. The call has been received, the connection has been made and by opening my heart to receive the answer, my light can return to the earth plane, to this body.

Within the heart are the patterns of existence through all time and space, and the answer it seeks is the light from its original intention. The purist light that holds within its stream the wisdom of the ages and the power of remembering. The hands begging and empty with light falling on them, cannot feed the yearning of a hungry heart.

For the heart is a magical place and the spark within it can light up a universe, illuminating to the rim, seeing all that is with curiosity and wonder. And so I open my arms and embrace this magical place of earth, for it has been in the dark for a long long time, and the light in my heart needs to shine upon the magic in order to illuminate its existence.

In every sunrise, life awakens to a new day, a different day, yesterday is gone and today has blue skies and the golden yellow ray of hope and joy. It is here, with this light, that my prayers have been answered. I feel the warmth of the sun's rays melting away the darkness.

I am loved. I allow myself to be loved. I am the BeLoved.

The Disciple - *being disciplined*

Within the centre of each heart exists the spark of our creation, bright as an inextinguishable star. This spark that lights the fire, keeps us warm and gives us light. Within each heart no matter the darkness, this spark of creation exists. As the light grows, more can be seen. Dedication to growing this light is a discipline, it is about becoming a disciple of the heart.

Within each heart are many stories, images and encounters of the day. These experiences send messages to the heart and create patterns of a reality that may be called 'the friends that we choose to hang out with.'

Inside the home of the heart exists each person's unique creation of chosen teachings and experiences for that soul to evolve.

Herein lives our personal power, to choose a reality of our own creation, feet firmly on the ground.

When the mental body is filled with images and stories outside of our own creation, it is simply the mental body. Should the heart choose to follow these stories, it can potentially become a betrayal of Self.

Finding that which brings joy, peace and love to each of our individual hearts is a unique experience to each soul. These choices of 'attention' are a discipline. To choose to be a disciple of one's own heart takes focus and will power, for there are many distractions along the way, seeking our attention.

Planting the Garden of Eden, creating a paradise for ourselves takes care, love and dedication. Attention to one's own garden and the seeds we plant, water and give energy to, is a choice of free will.

Our Garden of Eden grows from the soil up into the light with an abundance of green leaves, wild scented flowers and fruits in different flavours and colours.

This exquisite place of abundance feeds the body and the soul, and many birds visit and live here, parts of ourselves that are both on and off the earth-plane. As we root and ground ourselves into the earth, merging with her depths, we are able to grow higher into the light stretching ourselves beyond the blue skies into the dark, unknown surrounding universe, where the light and patterns of the stars are the designs of our creation.

The Dice - *aligning our heart with our truth, when creating*

The dice fall, seemingly by chance but in essence, within the flow of the unseen patterns under the hand. Sometimes the hand casts the dice to fall into a complete number twelve, the highest vibration possible. It never throws a zero, there is never the option of nothing. The play between the hands, the heart and the descending patterns from above, are the will of the soul.

By simply placing the right hand over the heart, and breathing into truth, asking the heart for its true story of creation in any given circumstance or situation, one can predict the outcome.

The closer the frequency of the heart in truth to the will of the hand, the more likely the given outcome. The universe is that which is the truth of the heart held in the palm of the hand, held under the light of creation, in the flow of the design of the Creator.

The Temple - *a sacred space within the heart*

Floating within the expansive blue skies of the heavens exists a temple of my own creation. The inner architecture reveals arches with paintings on the walls, stained glass windows and crystalline floors. Statues of the founding designs hold and support me, and carved white marble Angels abound. The pictures in the paintings tell the stories of my creation; the light inside this structure is alive and well. Resilient.

I feel as a child, sitting cross legged in the centre of the container, feeling and seeing with awe and wonder. This is a safe, exquisitely peaceful and pure place where I can visit at any time. It helps me to remember myself, beyond the life upon the busy streets thronging with crossways and intersections of human bodies, all with a purpose.

As I sit here, as the pure, innocent and trusting little girl, I behold this pure space around me, absorbing it into my heart. It gives me strength and knowing of those that have walked before and found their way home.

With many lifetimes on earth, the heart holds wisdom and truth that guides our soul forward.

The feelings in every situation connect us to remembering our higher wisdom and knowledge, from many lives of experience. With every beat of the heart, a pulse of energy expands outwards transmitting a frequency, and if the heart is open to receive, a response returns.

Within each of us is a voice in our heart, that speaks with truth, a voice we trust. But to hear this voice one must listen with a different ear, an inward ear that is held within the breath.

The individual heart is linked, united with the earth's heart, her wisdom is our wisdom, the wisdom of the collective. She knows. The inner ear hears this voice of the mother, Mother Earth, the mother consciousness within ourselves that cares, loves, nurtures and nourishes us. For our hearts are One.

Within each heart is a temple, a holy space where there is stillness and joy. And surrounding the temple is earth and sky, the blue heavens. One has travelled far to seek this holy space. Sometimes gatherings happen here, a coming together of souls to remember and connect. These heartfelt connections are deep and meaningful, helping us to understand this experience of life with its high's, low's and everything in between. The hum of quiet voices in the holy space is consolation, comfort to an alienated heart, a heart yearning to remember home; a seeking heart.

In this space the hearts are one and there is one dream, one vision. With the prosperity of mother nature on our side whilst we hold deep faith and trust, these yearning hearts will bring 'home' to the earth plane. That magical place where I am now. Within my heart...

The Deck of Cards and the Forest - *the potential house of numbers we can build as an experience to learn from, using the archetypes. We do this as individuals and as a collective, like trees in a forest*

Note: At the end of this story, a clear explanation of the archetypes and references can be found. The explanation acts as a guide, breaking down each aspect of an archetype and landscape as it relates to the story and our consciousness.

The Serpent in the Forest, large and black, lazy and slow, could be found with his companion, an older white haired man with twinkly blue eyes, holding a deck of cards in his hands. Shuffling the deck whilst standing next to the serpent the man casually questioned, 'I wonder how the deck will fall today, Sam?'

In his mind's eye he saw himself having built an upright castle with the deck, and then watched it collapse onto the table.

'Let me lay the cards out and see what the future predicts, for is there not divine mathematics to this universe? I read the numbers as if I were reading a storybook, seeing the steps unfold with numerical precision. What shall we do, Sam, with the predictability of this day? Reading the outcome makes me laugh. And you, you have become lazy with acceptance. What if we should build a house of cards which can withstand the highest wind, firm in its convictions with a dream of creation. A house that the rain, thunder and lightning can flow over without affect, untouched by the wind, steady and true. What if we build a house of cards like that, Sam? On this gloriously beautiful clear day, with its bright blue skies and deep stillness. Here on the table before me under this simple roof in the forest'.

The serpent listened attentively with a sly lift to the lip and a distant calculating glint in his eye, for his comfortable, lazy life was always foremost in his thoughts. His self serving approach to existence was one with the beat of his heart. He continued to observe this master holding the deck of cards between his hands, who was an amusing and powerful man and enjoyed the creative flair with which he controlled the deck, building and rebuilding houses, and always with curious wonder at how they might fall.

The master wondered, 'How does one build a house of cards that can withstand the elements of nature? A house that can also stand firmly in a breath of wind? It's simple,' he thought. 'I need to understand the nature of the elements so that I can use them to my advantage, so that this house can become untouchable.' 'Wonderful!' he congratulated himself, ' as One within the magical kingdom of the nature spirits and a house of my own that is untouchable'. He laid down the first card and placed it in the centre of the table facing upwards, it was the King of Hearts. He felt into his own heart for the strength and power of the King, unstoppable and ruling over his kingdom with majestic flow and creativity. Yes, this was the foundation of his house. He placed a second card upright on the Eastern side of the King, facing inwards, it was the Ace of Spades confirming that to build a new beginning in alignment with the dawning of a new day, he would need a spade to build a firm foundation. He loved the shape of the card, a heart with a handle, a heart that knows how to work.

On the West side of the King, the side of the setting sun at the completion of the day, he took a third card from the top of the deck, the Ace of Hearts and once again placed it facing inwards. 'Yes,' he thought 'a heart that knows of suffering and whose primary focus is to prevent these conditions.' To the North, the Queen of spades, a hard working queen with an understanding of her own heart. A queen whose focus is forwards and who is capable of digging a hole and burying anything in the way. And in the South the two of hearts, with the two of spades on top of it. For a balanced heart, a heart that understands the trials of the past as to influence our choices for the future and affect the work we are willing to do, guiding the way. A heart that has been pummelled and bruised, beaten into submission so that balance can be sought at all costs.

'Yes, this is going well,' he thought, and continued to build. 'It should be simple if I can connect these numbers to the nature of the forest. Align each number to that which resonates with it for greatest effect. The two of Spades will be the Eagle, its wings providing vision and balance to be able to see what needs to be done next. The Ace of Hearts will be the serpent slithering along the forest floor, lazily seeking edibles, its primary focus being to feed itself. The rabbit will be the four of clubs with its three leaves, giving balance in numbers.'

The Master gazed upon the house of cards with satisfaction, this was going well. Oh, the infinite possibilities and outcomes of different combinations. He stayed focused with his intention. As One with nature, an indestructible building.

Bowing his head to his heart he closed his eyes, and took a deep in-breath. 'Where in my heart is the roof, that which will protect the interior of the building?' he contemplated. He imagined ceramic tiles over a building under a blue sky, it could have been a villa in the countryside in Tuscany.

Then he knew it, the nine of clubs, the three leaves perfectly balanced and the number of completions covering the structure convincingly. Yes, all was well and in order and this seemed a solid form.

He sought in his heart the nature spirit that would fit with the nine and saw the crocodile, the reptilian part of the brain that absorbs all that it experiences. What better protection for his plan than the unconscious pattern of awareness of all that surrounds it. Completion of an indestructible plan that he would creatively implement for himself and his lazy slithering companion, that they could continue their simple and fortuitous lifestyle with individual satisfaction.

Let us enter the reptilian part of the brain, that part of ourselves that protects us. We begin with the crocodile, the perceived roof of the house. That part which appears to protect us from the rain, the sun, the wind and the storms, from that which we fear might damage our interiors. For nature can be quite outspoken when rebalancing herself.

When there is too much rain, the sun needs to come out and dry it up and when there is too much sun, the rain needs to supply water to the crusty earth for new life to grow. Nature, she is a sensitive and expressive Being. And she simply loves to finish with a splash of colour swirled across the sky, in the still aftermath of a storm.

The crocodile lived well between the land and the waters, absorbing the feelings of all that was around it and storing it in memory. And this was useful, for it could be referred to at any time and served as protection from the weather, just like the roof of the house. It learned the cause of changing weather conditions and eventually, was able to make predictions. Always remembering that a rainbow would complete the story. Knowing far in the back of its mind when to escape to a cave alongside the river, where the currents of overwhelm could sweep past it, whilst itself remained unaffected within the peaceful dark interior. Slowly, it receded into the stillness of the cave and submerged itself under the waters, reading nature and predicting an outcome, coming out for a sunny day to dry out and warm its scales and then once again escaping to the cave in unpleasant conditions.

The design of this house with its protective roof would not easily crumble, but consideration needed to be given to a potentially destructive wind.

The Eagle soared over the landscape of trees below, a dense green jungle, he sought a tall tree with no leaves that he might be close to the jungle with unhindered vision. He glided onto a branch, settled himself and listened attentively to the cacophony of sounds below, what seemed to be the noise of life without distinction. All the creatures in the forest needed to speak, for why else would they have a voice? He settled into silence letting the reverberation of sound echo through him. There was a pattern in the noisy chorus, a single voice within the many. The soul of the forest had a song, and it was an expression of great joy at simply Being, in expression of itself.

Yes, all was well in this world and so he pressed down upon his wings and lifted himself powerfully into the air. He ascended higher and higher until he felt the wind currents carrying him within the patterns of perfection. He was soaring within an expanse of ostensible emptiness. In this moment, nothing but endless blue space.

Closing his eyes, he felt the wind beneath his wings and came into awareness of the patterns of creation he was smoothly gliding along. The blue sky held the invisible designs of creation within its currents, of all that is and ever has been.

He opened his eyes and saw a mountain, a firm place on which to pause where the density beneath him would be unmovable in the most forceful of winds. Taking a breath he became aware of his beating heart, himself so powerful and light with the gift of higher vision and an intrinsic knowing of the unseen patterns of perfection.

He felt into the rhythm of his heart, and within lay the knowledge of a great wind approaching, he must seek shelter immediately. He swooped down to the river and sought a cave. The same cave as the crocodile, would provide shelter from the storm.

The King looked down on the table at the House of cards, 'where was the sun?' In his mind's eye he saw the Tarot card of the Sun and felt warmed by its presence. The Blue background surrounds the picture of a sun, so still and radiant. But this picture was very quickly replaced by that of a man in robes travelling alone down a dusty road, his robes being blown by a powerful wind.

The King could feel his inner struggle, grappling to stay upright and focused on a direction, the strength of the wind repeatedly sweeping him off course, and the cold slowly creeping in. The wind was creating chaos and he was struggling to focus. Why was he on this path and where was he going, he thought, pulling his robes closer for warmth. He tried to feel into his heart to remember, to seek a glimpse of light, a glow of warmth that could guide him forwards.

Clutching at his robes he connected his mind to his heart and imagined his destination, one step in front of the other was all that he could manage but all that he needed. The sun was setting behind him, the darkness creeping stealthily closer, the only light a glimmer of hope deep within the cave of his heart. How could he possibly stay on course in the dark with this crazy wind, he wondered.

As is the nature of the earthplane, once the sun had set the wind began to still, and there was slight reprieve from the insanity. He took a deep breath and sensed the stars above, shining their light onto him, guiding him, and soon he realised that it was almost easier to find direction in the dark with such clear patterning surrounding him. He felt into the reflection of the stars on his body, and it was as if he were walking on a map, the pathway before him as clear as the mirroring of a full moon's reflection upon the ocean.

The King of Hearts, the empowerment of Love reflected in the universe around him on this dark night of his soul - such a clear map, such a clear night. And in the silence only the sounds of his footsteps.

Explanation:

The deck of cards represents the infinite number of choices one can make, each with its own experience and teachings. Within the order there can be chaos, yet everything is always in perfection. The house of cards is any given house that we create for a chosen experience.

The serpent is the kundalini energy or life force of an individual or collective.

The elements are the individual and collective condition of Being. Where earth is the physical body, wind the mental body, and the rain would refer to the emotional body.

The crocodile holds the patterns within the reptilian part of the brain, controlling consciousness through fear, whilst the eagle has higher vision on how to go forward.

The rainbow are the balanced chakras aligning in a circular stream of white light.

The wind would be interference within the mental body at an individual or collective level.

The eagle has the ability of higher vision and also the gift of landing perspective within the physical body, the patterning of the tree of life. Higher perspective from lifetimes of earthly experience. This is connected to the wisdom of the mountains, that deep knowing in the body holding the patterns of the original designs that have materialised and densified over eons of time.

The mighty wind refers to disruption in the mental body. The causes of this are many and may include, manipulation by the media, chemicals, mental addiction and disempowerment to programming, old stories or belief systems, and anything else that creates disturbance in the mind.

Yet, within the darkness, within the deep unconscious, exists the patterns of the stars, the original design of our creation as the universe. And when we seek within our own darkness we return to this design.

Landscapes of Consciousness in Form

As above, so below.

The peaceful tones of a great lake, with the waters reflecting a muted sky and merging horizon. A mirror, and perfect expression of the Creator in form.

Upon the lake a mighty crystalline circle contains patterns of cycles and circles, which occasionally fragment and then reconnect within the ripples on the surface.

The patterns emanate from and descend into the water in diamond crystalline geometries of light, transparent perfection which steadily subsides into the depths beneath. Here they will embody into the earth. Clear mineral embedded within structure.

As the patterns subside into the dark depths of the lake, their illuminating light-forms dissolve murky unseen areas, bringing clarity and transparency. The patterns glow into the steadily clearing waters and the skies above begin to reflect boundless blue.

Above the water, shimmering light configurations descend from above, sparkles of mirrored reflection, glimmers of hope between dimensions of time and space. This merging of design between air and water is pure clarity descending from the highest and the holiest.

Such is the experience between the mind and emotional body as consciousness settles into form. With deep breaths of trust and acceptance, the knowing hand of the Creator arrives, the breath connecting the body to its mighty director. With each inhalation of light patterned perfection, the body unites with the heavens, becoming an expression of the Divine.

The soils of the earth appear rich and dark with life. They are solid matter from which the descending light expresses itself into form. Growth reaching upwards into the light, absorbing the patterns and breathing them into designs of colour and sound, each a unique individual expression of magnificence. Spirit in Form.

Gazing over the great lake of water into the distance, the horizon slowly separates and one can see beyond the daylight into an infinite night sky; where countless stars hold their individual orientation within the ever spinning cycles and circles of time.

Each star sends forth its unique frequency of design, a wave of perfect vibrational light, the spark of its intended creation a wondrous gift.

And this wave of light gently undulates through the darkness to arrive upon the earth plane as a perspective, seeing through the eyes of a life form.

It looks around and views an empty desert landscape.

Deepening into the memory of its heart, it recalls the green lush vegetation of vibrant life of the forest where balance exists. Where the rain nourishes abundant plant life and living creatures, and white butterflies joyfully flutter amongst the sweet sounds of birds, flying from tree to tree singing their stories of existence.

This ray of light is simply a part of it all.

In the heart of the forest with its dense green vegetation and high canopy of trees, the blue skies of the heavens seem elusive, merely a glimpse of freedom here and there. Only the tallest trees are able to unite with the pure light of heaven and hear the uninterrupted stories of the wind.

A sturdy sequoia stands firm and tall, its roots embedded into the dark soils below, balancing its triangular frame. The roots extend deeply into the darkness seeking the gentle coloured vibrations of the soft pink rocks between the compressed particles, finding strength in these solidified gifts of compassion. For between the living soil, solid rose quartz pieces, exude waves of loving light that can also be seen in the sunset and sunrise on the horizon above, where the landscape is open and the winds of song pass softly by.

The tree is surrounded by dense growth, prickly sticks and thorns making it almost inaccessible. This form of protection permits it to grow tall and strong, its inner veins of flow transmitting messages of connection between the light of the blue heavens and the dark sturdy earth beneath. Its position in the forest is a placement of perfect orientation for the connections around it, its heart beating in concentric circles outwards, reaching all of the forest and beyond. The pulsing circles are united with the heartbeat of the earth, rhythmically expanding outwards.

The tree stands steady and still, a receptor and transmitter of light and sound, its vertical flow up and down a response between the heavens and the earth. This pattern of the tree of life is a communicative interface between the worlds.

Another tree stands alone between rolling green hills in the late afternoon sunlight. It stands on undulating waves of materialised green heart light, that separate the earth and the skies. The soft golden light bounces off the green leaves of the tree warmly, lovingly allowing the leaves to receive and transmute the light into food for its branches, body and roots. The tree receives this light unconditionally, trusting its frequencies of connection. The roots quiver with the messages of light, serpentine waves of nerve endings transmitting messages to the heart beneath, the earth's core. A pink heart of compassion covered in veins of flowing rivers and streams.

Each vein appears as blue as the heavenly skies, enclosed within a membrane of filmy protection.

A white cloud in the sky drifts alone, as if forgotten and without purpose. It contains the potential for lightning and thunder within its nature, a consequence of a prospective environment. The nature of the cloud holds the potential experience for both expansion and destruction as well as evaporation, depending on the conditions of its environment, how it has developed and the direction in which it is moving.

The tops of the mountains are frequently covered in misty clouds, their lofty wisdom concealed despite their deep connection into the earth. For the mountains have been pushed to great heights from turbulent depths. Within the mists of time unseen, lies the wisdom of the past written into the body, the very material structure of our being, a memory upholding all of existence. The lavender blue mountain tops erupt into the azure skies, cutting into the horizon with sharp serrated edges. Their majestic height and immutable strength are a force capable of withstanding the most destructive elements of the earth's terrain. Storms come and go and the mountains appear unmoved, their compact structure resisting corruption. Above and below the horizon, a perfect balance.

Rose quartz crystals lie randomly strewn across the empty desert lands, the sands of time shifting and moving in waves across the barren landscape, under infinite blue skies. Their crystalline, soft- pink vibrations, emanate from the surface of the hard dry plane. They rest serenely between heaven and earth on the surface of above and below. Pink crystalline hearts of compassion, steadfastly between.

Seeking Life on Earth

Within each of our hearts is the darkness that is, the darkness that we have chosen to learn from. We explore this emptiness seeking something where there is nothing. And when the emptiness, the meaningless existence of that seeking and searching is complete, we withdraw our curiosity back into the light. That which can be seen.

For although the seen world may feel boring, it is nevertheless the tangible form of the materialised world around us. When darkness begins to take form, the distortions in physical appearance become evident, and this is boring too. It is simply the seeking within the unknown, within the mystery that excites us and holds our curiosity.

Within the light at higher levels there is a magical existence, a frequency of activity that exists and is infinitely wonderful in its creation. The chatter of vibrant colours and patterns, creatures of nature, of the natural world all living in harmony, all singing in a chorus of song.

Tuning into this frequency of light takes will power and perseverance, it is a harmonic merging. And this is a practice in one's heart, to find this frequency of Love, this resonation. To discover the magic of the earth plane once again, this life in the light. The Aliveness of Being Here.

Soul Return

The Earth floated in space with the universe supporting her, the patterns of the stars in designs of perfection surrounding her. A serpent of wisdom travelled through space finding its way, discovering a pathway through every barrier with perseverance, its intention to return.

She arrived at the crystalline doorway to the earth-plane where there was nothing but emptiness to welcome her. Although she was too large for the entrance she saw through the archway deep into the mists of time. Clouds floating in various densities, layers of gentle pastel colours with many pink hue's reflecting off their foggy particles. And each particle, a perfect sphere scattering the reflection of the fading light, soft and complete.

Her ever shifting tongue flickered, testing the frequencies on the other side of the doorway, tasting and absorbing the information within the light's vibrations.

Inhaling deeply, she shifted the width of her body into length and slid carefully through the entranceway. Returning to her original shape on the other side, she breathed in the light, absorbing it through her mouth as well as her entire Being. Merging with her surroundings she soaked in the reflections from the particles of water.

Attentively, she examined the layers of consciousness beneath her. She sought within the separated frequencies, she was seeking the space from which she had heard and responded to the call.

The mists began to dissolve and below her to the front at exactly 13.04, an island appeared surrounded by water. She descended, moving forwards in sideway oscillations.

As she materialised onto the island she held her awareness of the clear blue skies above her and the perfection of her landing, noting the infinity 8 completing its course above her. Her large spirit felt tightly compressed into the much smaller body.

She made her way forwards.

This human form felt so delicate and breakable. She breathed into the earth below her feet, connecting to the serpent upward flow.

'I Am here,' she thought. This island and I are One, made of earth and supported by water.

Expanding her consciousness outwards she merged with the ocean and its ever shifting hue's of blues. Some were heavy and clouded while others were crystalline and transparent. And thus, she slowly deepened her feelings into the Truth of Being here. She noted the difference in density between the mass of water and the mists on high, aware that they were both the very same particles.

Feeling into the weight of her presence she lowered her vibration to a slow and steady pulse, to the heartbeat of the earth beneath her feet. She allowed this knowledge of Home to arrive.

Feeling into the anchored beat of her heart, she remembered the obstacles on her way down and gave herself a little shake, letting the memories of resistance fade and dissolve.

She felt into her hands with their ten fingers, each finger an emanation of light with a magical and infinite potential to create. The pulse in her heart flowed outwards through each fingertip connecting the sound, the voice of her heart to the nature spirits surrounding her. Gently she reached towards a flower, its open petals so delicate and vulnerable beneath her fingertips, so trusting and welcoming. The flowers' exquisite crystalline colours began to glow, responding to her presence. Connection.

Deep within the heart of the ocean was a cave wherein a man lived. A man who could speak the language of the waters, could sing lines of connection that were visible on the surface as waves.

Although he resided in the cave, there was in fact no separation between him and the ocean, they were One.

She greeted him seeing his nature with appreciation, and the twinkle in his blue eyes acknowledged her arrival. They would work well together.

Transformation - *I am the Butterfly*

A blanket of multi-coloured flowers covered the flat desert floor, life after the rain. A little caterpillar crawled determinedly eastwards, its full body ready to settle. The sun was speedily setting upon the horizon to the West, and the long shadows were becoming cool and gripping.

He centred within his heart and began with an earnest prayer of intention, that he might begin his process of spinning the light around himself before the sun disappeared. Locating a large, dark-green leaf he came to stillness. Then humming a tone from his heart-centre he united its beat with the Great Mothers rhythm. Holding his prayer within his expression, he began to spin the golden threads of protection around himself.

The desert night sounds emerged and the stars began to twinkle as he sang his song of creation into the surrounding threads. Before this night concluded and the sun rose to the East, his cocoon would be complete. Then he would surrender himself into the liquid state releasing his crawling form, to be re-patterned by the stars that he might be free to fly. His heart felt light and hopeful as the silvery threads of light from the stars shone upon him through the darkness. And he received these light threads, becoming their sound, becoming their song. And as the night continued and the spirals of golden-white light whirled across the skies, he united with their chorus and his wings slowly emerged.

Warm fingers of golden light stretched across the level desert sands, unveiling bountiful rainbow-crystalline circles hovering above the flowers. Circles and cycles of evolution, all connected in varying sizes and levels of being. And the large blue butterfly gently flapped his wings travelling through it all.

The Carousel - the Purelands of Amitabha

All of the lives I have lived are all of the legs of the millipede to walk with and depend upon. To stand upon. Those lives have given me strength and understanding of the freedom and playground that this earth plane is. And although I have swung to the edges of my reality peering into the dark spaces beyond, I have not let go.

Imagine my consideration to relinquish my grip on the handle-bar of my swing, attached to the merry-go-round of this circus? To free-fall into space? It feels like the ultimate trust and freedom of the dark unknown.

The circles and cycles of the circus carousel are eternal, and to release the hand that grips the handlebar whilst leaning over the edge, is to fearlessly fly off. It is to trust that within the empty dark space of nothingness and emptiness is where true freedom draws breath.

I am holding fearfully onto the handlebar of an ever spinning wheel, rotating in endless cycles and circles, alternating my hands and occasionally leaning backwards to hold the bar with both hands.

There must always be something to hold onto.

Until nauseous and dizzy I arrive at the seemingly pointless purpose of the exercise.

Finally,

I surrender and let go, flying off the edge into the perceived empty darkness. And within that emptiness, floating everywhere and nowhere in the breath, there is a deep comfort of being held.

Supported as myself.

Supported as 'I Am.'

ACKNOWLEDGEMENTS

Thank you to both of my children for being my earthlines. My beloved daughter, for her love and earthly wisdom, who always supports and helps to make this work understandable and cohesive.

My beloved son, for his love and teaching me the meaning of trust. To my birth family, thank you for allowing me to be myself, simply watching it all unfold with a remarkable amount of acceptance.

With enormous appreciation for all of my very patient clients. I am so grateful for your support throughout this process as we learned together. When I faltered, lacking courage and trust, it was you who carried our journey for me. These writings are our reflection.

Great Spirit. I would like to acknowledge those that I am aware have guided my journey. There are many that are unseen and have stood by supporting my process and I thank all that I am in consciousness, both awake and asleep to.

My 'house' includes Mother/Father God; my ancestors; my master teachers and guides; including Master Orlando whom I have not met but is alive on the earthplane and Master Hilario just off the earth plane, both have taught me much about surgeries and uniting our bodies with the elemental kingdom; Master Rosendo Pisario for the power of prayers; the Star Nations with the Galactic Federation, the Galactic Council and Ashtar of the Command, for their protection and guidance; the Vedas with special mention of Ganesha; the Tibetans with the Dalai Lama who has been with me since I was a child; the Temple of the Buddha; the Masters of the Rays; the Biblical Masters and those from the Far East; the Mahatma; the House of Ka; Mother Mary; Mother Quan Yin; the Angelic and Archangelic Kingdoms; the Elemental Kingdom, the Devic Kingdom, the Elohim and the Avatars. With all of this guidance, the 'House' that I return and unite myself with, is my Home, Mother Earth. My purpose being to unite myself and other willing souls with the blueprint design of her nature, that I can remember all of my lifetimes upon her and what I have learned here. This book is some of the designs that I understand from my experience of being here. I hope that they will help you remember our home that we created here, too.

Key Words

CROSS IN THE CIRCLE - our astrological earth symbol, balance between the lower four bodies bringing vertical alignment.

Earth - physical body

Water - emotional body

Air - mental body

Fire - spirit body

West - completion

East - new beginnings,

North - Future, original design of creation

South - past, experience

Nighttime - unconscious

Daytime - conscious

Garden of Eden/Paradise/Blueprint - patterns of perfection found in the Tree of life, Flower of life, seed of life and fruit of life

Mountain - embodied wisdom

Cave - earthly heart or natural space in the mountain, where our wisdom resides

Sand - sands of time, lifetimes on the earth plane held within the DNA

River - connection to the flow of life, from the mountains of wisdom to the ocean of oneness through the many landscapes of earthly existence

Ocean - emotional connection to the oneness of all life

Tree - the tree of life geometry within the cells of the body as key to our divine nature

Mother Nature - green of the heart chakra, our divine nature

Rainbow - balance of the chakras, completion of a story

White - purity and innocence, aligned chakras

Pot of gold - Wealth of mother earth and golden age of light, our return and connection to the knowing of ourselves as love. Golden light materialises into gold.

UFO - vehicle of light of an extra-terrestrial nature

Carriage - vehicle of light

Serpent/Kundalini - life force, moves forward in oscillations of west and east

Angels - messengers bringing messages from the higher realms, intuition

Bird - part of the spirit that has wings and knows how to fly

Cats - courage

Crocodile - reptilian or primal part of the brain that controls self preservation

Hippo - emotional defensive aggressiveness

Rhino - embodied (white)defensive aggressiveness or (black)aggressive defensiveness

Giraffe - higher perspective on the earth plane.

Eagle - higher vision

Horses - power/horsepower

Owl - wise elder, wisdom

Stork - new beginnings

Unicorn - power and vision

Spider - creator of connection or disconnection through a web

Locust - something that plagues one

Dragon - power, has all four bodies, walks on the earth, swims in the water, flies in the air and has the breath of fire

Pine trees - crystalline, christ-aligned consciousness

Blue sky - conscious awareness

Night Sky - design of our creation, blueprint

Father Christmas - father of christ consciousness

Mother Mary - the Great mother that birthed crystalline consciousness

The little Girl - trust ourselves to receive the light that we are, pure and innocent

The little Boy - trusting ourselves to give ourselves what we need

Flower - the pattern in the heart of our perfect design

Walking stick - crutch

Staff - tree of life connection, conscious wisdom

Blue - willpower

Pink - compassion

Gold - wisdom

Fleur de lis - empowerment to move forward as seen as a key on Royal Fabric

Three fold flame - transformation through the pink, gold and blue flames of light

Sunset - completion through transcendence of the pink, blue and gold

Sunrise - new beginnings through evolution of balance through balanced pink, blue and gold

First dimension - Sunset - Completion

Second dimension - Sunrise - New Beginnings

Third Dimension - magnification

Fourth Dimension - Flow

Fifth Dimension - Structure

Sixth Dimension - Ideal

Seventh Dimension - Expansion

Eighth Dimension - Potential

Ninth Dimension - Co-creation

Pearls - pearls of wisdom, pearlescent light

Flower - the flower of life design incorporating the patterns of perfection of our blueprint, also the circles and cycles of time

Tree - As above so below

Green rolling hills - waves of materialised earth heart chakra

King - self empowered masculine

Queen - self empowered feminine

Castle - home in our heart

Kingdom - surrounding the castle, kingdoms of heaven

DNA - ladder of connection, when activated becomes a three dimensional ascending/descending spiral staircase

Gold - the wealth of this planet and connects us to all that we are. Gold is a conductor and gives protection due to its reflective nature. Golden light materialises into gold.

Circles and Cycles - Colours correlate with the chakras. Red - base chakra, orange - sacral chakra, yellow - solar plexus, green - heart chakra, blue - throat chakra, indigo - third eye. The spinning rainbow of the chakras balances into a stream of white light, usually ending with the little girl standing on the pot of gold at the end of the rainbow. Connection to the Golden Age of Light.

Printed in Great Britain
by Amazon